**EXECUTIVE EDITORS**
Mike Mifsud, Alan Doan, Jenny Doan,
Sarah Galbraith, David Mifsud

**MANAGING EDITOR**
Natalie Earnheart

**CREATIVE DIRECTOR**
Christine Ricks

**PHOTOGRAPHY TEAM**
Mike Brunner, Lauren Dorton, Jennifer Dowling,
Dustin Weant

**PATTERN TEAM**
Edie McGinnis, Denise Lane, Jessica Woods,
Gregg Allnutt

**PROJECT DESIGN TEAM**
Natalie Earnheart, Jenny Doan

**EDITOR & COPYWRITERS**
Jenny Doan, Natalie Earnheart, Christine Ricks,
Katie Mifsud, Camille Maddox, Nichole Spravzoff,
Edie McGinnis

**SEWISTS TEAM**
Janet Yamamoto, Carol Henderson, Denise Lane,
Janice Richardson, Jamey Stone

**QUILTING & BINDING DEPARTMENT**
Sarah Richardson, Becky Bowen, Linda Frump, Nikki
LaPiana, Sandy Moss, Angela Wilson, Linda Frump,
Debbie Elder, Betty Bates, Karla Zinkand, Jan Meek,
Chelsea White, Debbie Allen, Charlene Ensz, Jamee
Gilgour, Stephanie Weaver, Christine Atteberry,
Natalie Loucks, Dennis Voss, Kara Snow, Devin
Ragle, Rachael Joyce, Bruce Van Iperen, Francesca
Flemming, Aaron Crawford, Ethan Lucas, Lyndia
Lovell, Cyera Cottrill, Salena Smiley, Deborah Warner,
Elizabeth Hostetler, Deloris Burnett, Bernice Kelly

**PRINTING COORDINATOR**
Rob Stoebener

**PRINTING SERVICES**
Walsworth Print Group
803 South Missouri
Marceline, MO 64658

**CONTACT US**
Missouri Star Quilt Company
114 N Davis
Hamilton, Mo. 64644
888-571-1122
info@missouriquiltco.com

# content

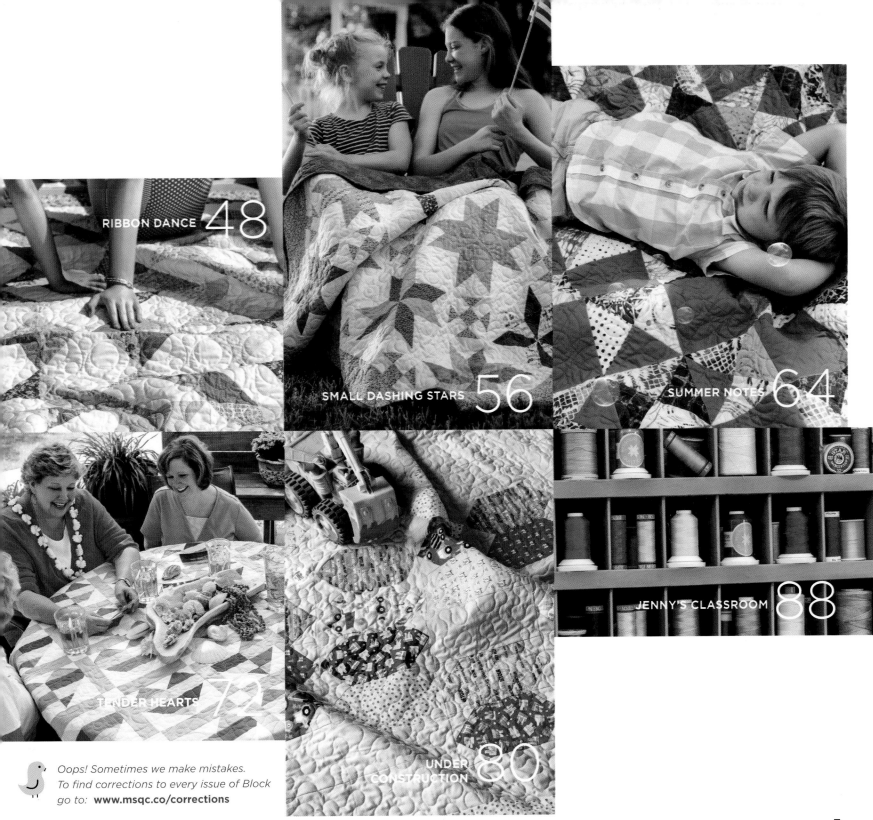

*Oops! Sometimes we make mistakes.
To find corrections to every issue of Block
go to:* **www.msqc.co/corrections**

# hello

As the lyrics of an old song go, "Summer breeze makes me feel fine." Being a California girl, I relish the warmer days and thrive in the sunshine. I can't contain my enthusiasm as the days get longer and the chill leaves the air. I bustle about the house opening windows and breathing in the earthy, sweet smell of the world blooming.

Summertime is all about relaxation and living life at a slower pace. There's always something to be done that can't be accomplished during the winter, but you'll excuse me if my flower beds get a little weed-ridden while I'm reading a book out on the porch or doing a bit of hand stitching. It's okay to let some things go.

When my kids were little, I rushed about trying to do so many things perfectly until a point where it became tedious. It affected my enjoyment of their childhood so I decided to stop. Life isn't meant to be lived in a museum. A few socks on the floor doesn't make the difference between a good or a bad day.

This summer, give yourself the gift of letting some things go. Pick up a fun project instead of a handful of weeds. You'll never regret slowing down and giving yourself some time to bask in the glory of the season.

JENNY DOAN
MISSOURI STAR QUILT CO

# TRY OUR APP

It's easy to keep up on every issue of BLOCK magazine. Access it from all your devices. And when you subscribe to BLOCK, it's free with your subscription!

# soak up the
# *sunshine*

Everything is green right now. The trees have filled in, the grass is lush and perfect for little toes to walk through. Irises, poppies and peonies are all blooming. The world around me sings with colors so rich and vibrant. These summer days are just begging me to park a quilt somewhere and soak up the sun. Amid these colorful surroundings it's easy to find inspiration for my quilting projects.

Have you ever tried sitting down with a pile of fabric and let it speak to you? Here's what I do. I start by placing some fabric in front of me. I close my eyes and take some deep breaths. With eyes still closed I allow myself to just sit there for a few minutes. I think about my project. What do I envision it becoming? What ideas do I typically lean toward? Am I open to exploring something new? Then I open my eyes and reach for the first few fabrics that strike my eye. I've recently been trying this each time I start a new project and I love the results. Amazingly, these unlikely combinations end up being some of my favorites. If you're looking for a new idea or challenge, try simply changing how you approach it. You just might surprise yourself!

CHRISTINE RICKS
*MSQC Creative Director, BLOCK MAGAZINE*

**PRINTS**

**FBY42980** Uppercase - Dotty Metallic Silver
by Janine Vangool for Windham Fabrics
SKU: 41823M-6

**FBY50906** Dominicana - Tonal Triangles
by Vanessa Vargas Wilson for Timeless Treasures
SKU: Fun-C3776 Yellow

**FBY53374** Juxtaposey - Posey Medallion Aqua
Yardage by Betz White for Riley Blake
SKU: C5922-AQUA

**FBY52661** Coney Island - Berry Medley Candy
Apple Red by Fig Tree & Co. (Joanna Figueroa)
for Moda Fabrics
SKU: 20287-12

**FBY30755** Katie Jump Rope - Daisy Bouquet Royal
by Denyse Schmidt for Free Spirit Fabrics
SKU: PWDS108.ROYAL

**FBY57244** Kimberbell Basics - Dotted Circles
Green Tonal by Kim Christopherson for
Maywood Studio
SKU: MAS8241-GG

**SOLIDS**

**FBY1168** Bella Solids - White Bleached
by Moda Fabrics
SKU: 9900 98

**FBY8514** Cotton Supreme Solids - Tourmaline
by RJR Fabrics
SKU: 9617 103

**FBY12136** Bella Solids - Caribbean
by Moda Fabrics
SKU: 9900 86

**FBY12154** Bella Solids - Popsicle
by Moda Fabrics
SKU: 9900 143

**FBY1686** Bella Solids - Admiral Blue
by Moda Fabrics
SKU: 9900 48

**FBY57824** Bella Solids - Basil
by Moda Fabrics
SKU: 9900 330

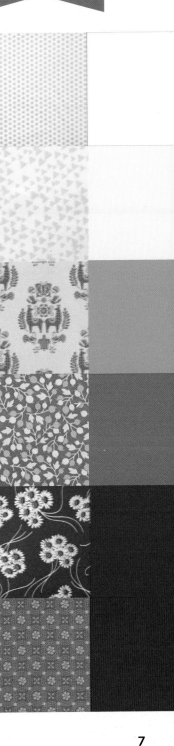

For the tutorial and everything you need to make this quilt visit:
**www.msqc.co/blocksummer17**

# all my Xs

My young friend, Anna, loved to go fishing with her family. Every summer their twelve-passenger van was packed to the gills with camping gear and fishing poles as they headed to the mountains for a long weekend in the woods.

Anna's mother wasn't much for fishing. She stayed at camp while Dad led the fishing expedition down to the water's edge. Five kids versus one adult can stretch the patience of even the most gentle of parents, but memories were more important than the number of fish in the basket, so down to the lake they went.

The year Anna turned eight, she decided she was big enough to cast her own line. Her dad tied on the hook and attached a little lure that looked like a shimmering yellow fish.

"Before you cast the line, make sure all is clear behind you," Dad cautioned. But Anna was a bit of a wanderer, and without even noticing, she ended up in a brushy stretch of shoreline with her hook caught in bushes.

Dad patiently helped her untangle the line, but before he could step out of the way, Anna stretched the pole back over her right shoulder, brought it forward with as much power as she could muster, and released that line like a pro. She expected to see the lure fly gracefully out over the water and land with a gentle plop, but it was stuck, most likely tangled in the scrubby bushes, she thought to herself. Determined to continue unassisted, Anna gave that line a powerful tug.

"Anna-girl, you've caught something, but it isn't a fish," Dad called out, laughing.

Anna was disappointed to discover that her hook had snagged the pocket flap of her father's red and black plaid flannel shirt. She was embarrassed, but giggled a simple apology as Daddy prepared the line to be cast once again.

She cast that line with all her might, never noticing that she had once again sidestepped her way into the path of trouble.

"Stop!" yelped Dad. "Anna, stop tugging the line!" There was a desperation in Dad's voice that Anna didn't like. She whipped around to face Dad. Her jaw dropped and she stared in disbelief at that shiny yellow lure stuck through the side of Dad's left nostril. A laugh escaped her lips but was quickly stifled by Dad's warning eyes. This was some serious business.

Upon inspection, it was discovered that the hook had made it's way completely through his nostril. The barb was securely fixed inside Dad's nose and there was no way to remove it without cutting off the barb. So there they were, in the middle of the woods, miles from a phone or a doctor—or a good pair of wire snips—and Dad had a two-inch-long fish lure dangling from his nose. Lucky for Anna, her dad is one patient man, and after a long drive to the ER and plenty of finagling, his nose was finally hook-free.

Many years have come and gone since that memorable fishing trip, but everyone still loves to hear the story of the time Dad got his nose pierced.

# materials

**QUILT SIZE**
69" X 78"

**BLOCK SIZE**
9" finished

**QUILT TOP**
1 package 10" print squares **or**
  4 matching packages of 5" print
  squares
4 yards background fabric – includes
  inner border

**OUTER BORDER**
1¼ yards

**BINDING**
¾ yard

**BACKING**
4¾ yards - vertical seam(s)

**SAMPLE QUILT**
**In the Limelight** by Wilmington
Batiks

# 1 cut

From the background fabric, cut:

- (39) 3" strips across the width
  of the fabric. Subcut the strips
  into 3" squares. Each strip will
  yield 13 squares and a **total of
  504** are needed. Set the
  remaining fabric aside for the
  inner border.

From the package of 10" print squares,
cut:

- (4) 5" squares from each for
  a **total of 168 squares.** Keep all
  matching prints together.

2A

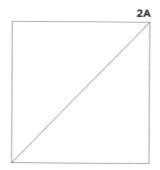

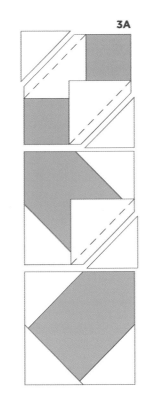

3A

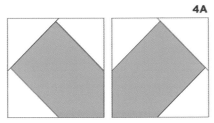

4A

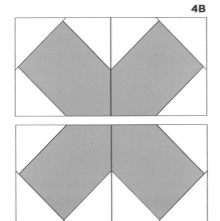

4B

## 2 mark

On the reverse side of the 3″ background squares, draw a line or press a crease from corner to corner once on the diagonal to mark a sewing line. 2A

## 3 snowball corners

Place a marked 3″ background square on 2 opposite corners of a 5″ square with right sides facing. Sew on the marked line. Trim the excess fabric away ¼″ from the sewn seam and press. Place another 3″ marked background square on 1 of the remaining corners and sew on the marked line. Trim the excess fabric away ¼″ from the sewn seam and press. Keep all matching prints together. **Make 168 units.** 3A

## 4 block construction

Sew 2 rows of 2 matching print units together as shown. Notice how each unit is positioned. 4A

Sew the 2 rows together to complete the block. **Make 42.** 4B

**Block Size:** 9″ finished

## 5 arrange and sew

Lay out the blocks in **7 rows** with each row having **6 blocks.** When satisfied with the appearance, sew the blocks together to make a row. Press the seam allowances in the odd-numbered rows toward the left and the even-numbered rows toward the right to make the corners of each block nest easily. Sew the rows together.

## 6 inner border

Cut (7) 2½″ strips across the width of fabric of the remaining background fabric. Sew them together end-to-end to make one long strip. Trim the borders from this strip.

Refer to Borders (pg. 103) in the Construction Basics to measure and cut the inner borders. The strips are approximately 63½″ for the sides and approximately 58½″ for the top and bottom.

## 7 outer border

Cut (7) 6″ strips across the width of the fabric. Sew the strips together end-to-end to make one long strip. Trim the borders from this strip.

Refer to Borders (pg. 103) in the Construction Basics to measure and cut the outer borders. The strips are approximately 67½″ for the sides and approximately 69½″ for the top and bottom.

## 8 quilt and bind

Layer the quilt with batting and backing and quilt. After the quilting is complete, square up the quilt and trim away all excess batting and backing. Add binding to complete the quilt. See Construction Basics (pg. 103) for binding instructions.

1 On the reverse side of each of the 3″ background squares, draw a line from corner to corner once on the diagonal or press a crease in place to mark a sewing line.

2 Place a marked 3″ background square on 2 opposite corners of a 5″ square with right sides facing. Sew on the marked line then trim ¼″ away from the sewn seams.

3 Place another 3″ marked square on 1 of the remaining corners and sew on the marked line. Trim the excess fabric away ¼″ from the sewn seam and press. Make 4.

4 Sew 2 matching quadrants together to make a row. Make 2 rows then sew the rows together to complete 1 block.

# cascade
## *quilt*

Yellowstone National Park is a vast and beautiful place. Oh, it can get pretty busy with campers and tour buses, but if you venture off the beaten path, there are over two million acres of wilderness just waiting to be explored.

I knew a cute Midwestern gal who dreamed of visiting Yellowstone from the time she was a little girl. Growing up, Bev's family never had enough money to make the trip, but she pored over travel guides, dreaming of rainbow-hued geysers and herds of wild bison.

When Bev got married, she and her husband had big plans to roadtrip their way to the park, but those early years were all a whirl with college, babies, new careers, and bills.

Finally, when Bev's two daughters were young teens, the family decided to make the trip. Unfortunately, Bev's husband had to stay home to solve a last-minute work emergency, so they decided to make it a girls' trip.

Bev filled the minivan with sleeping bags, marshmallow roasting sticks, and a detailed daily agenda. With only one week to fulfill the dream of a lifetime, every moment counted!

It took nearly twenty-four hours to travel from Bev's Indiana home to Yellowstone. As they rolled into the campsite, Bev couldn't help but notice the many bear warning signs.

For the tutorial and everything
you need to make this quilt visit:
**www.msqc.co/blocksummer17**

They pitched the tent, roasted hot dogs for dinner, and cleaned up for the night. The ranger had cautioned them to keep all scented items—lotion, deodorant, snacks, soap —in the campsite's large, metal, bear-proof storage box. If it had a smell, it had the potential to attract bears, so in the box it went.

Once everything was safely locked away, Bev snuggled down into her sleeping bag and closed her eyes. Suddenly, she smelled something sweet. Her eyes flew open. "What is that? What is that smell?" she cried out.

"It's my chapstick, Mom! I'm sorry! I didn't even think about it! My lips were sooo dry!" her daughter responded.

In Bev's mind, they were goners. After all their efforts to stay safe from bear attacks, it seemed thirteen-year-old Jackie had sealed their fate with a little tube of lip gloss.

All through the night they lay motionless, eyes wide open and ears straining to hear the rustle of a hungry bear. Morning came, and by some miracle, they had survived!

The rest of the week was a dream come true with majestic vistas and adventure at every turn. And, of course, that chapstick spent each and every night tucked carefully into the bear box.

# materials

### QUILT SIZE
76½" X 89"

### BLOCK SIZE
13½" x 4" finished

### QUILT TOP
1 roll of 2½" print strips
1 roll of 2½" background strips
  **or** 3 yards background fabric cut into
  (40) 2½" x width of fabric strips

### BORDER
1¼ yards

### BINDING
¾ yard

### BACKING
2½ yards 108" wide

### OTHER SUPPLIES
The Binding Tool by TQM Products

### SAMPLE QUILT
**Faded Memories** by Geri Robins for
Penny Rose Fabrics

# 1 cut

Open the roll of print strips. Cut each
strip into (5) 8⅜" rectangles. Stack the
rectangles one atop the other with all
fabrics right side up. Place the binding
tool on top of a stack of 4 – 5 pieces and
cut the angle. **1A**

**NOTE:** *All pieces must be cut
exactly the same, at the same
angle! Repeat for all the strips in
the roll. You will have a **total of
200** print pieces.*

**1A**

**1B**

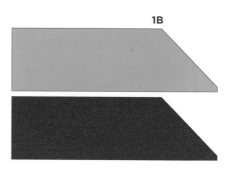

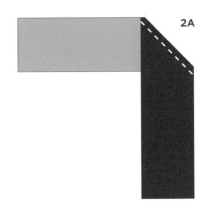

**2A**

Repeat the cutting directions on pg. 20 for the roll of background strips. Remember each piece must be cut exactly the same as the print pieces, right side up and at the same angle. Cut a **total of 200** pieces. 1B

## 2 sew

Align the angled edge of a print rectangle with the angled edge of a background rectangle with right sides facing. Using a ¼" seam allowance, sew the two pieces together along the angle. 2A

Open and press toward the darker fabric. **Make 2.** 2B

**2B**

Sew the 2 pieces together as shown to complete the block. **Make 100.** 2C

**Block Size:** 13½" x 4" finished

## 3 arrange in rows

Lay out the blocks in rows, with each row having **5 blocks**. Sew the blocks together. **Make 20 rows.** Press the seam allowances in the even rows toward the left and the odd rows toward the right. This will make the seams "nest" together and the corners match more easily. Sew the rows together.

**2C**

## 4 border

Cut (8) 5" strips across the width of the fabric. Sew the strips together end-to-end to make one long strip. Trim the borders from this strip.

Refer to Borders (pg. 103) in the Construction Basics to measure and cut the outer borders. The strips are approximately 80½" for the sides and approximately 77" for the top and bottom.

## 5 quilt and bind

Layer the quilt with batting and backing and quilt. After the quilting is complete, square up the quilt and trim away all excess batting and backing. Add binding to complete the quilt. See Construction Basics (pg. 103) for binding instructions.

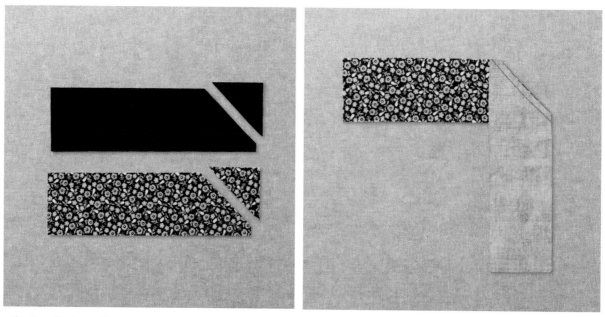

1 Cut all print and background strips into (5) 8⅜"
rectangles. Stack the rectangles one atop the other
with all fabrics right side up. Place the binding tool
on top of a stack of 4 – 5 pieces and cut the angle.
All pieces must be cut exactly the same.

2 Align the angled edge of a print rectangle with the
angled edge of a background rectangle with right sides
facing. Sew the 2 pieces together along the angle using
a ¼" seam allowance.

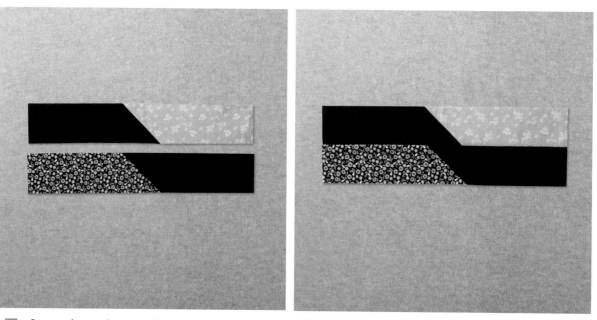

3 Open and press the seam allowances toward the
darker fabric. Sew the 2 pieces together as shown
to complete one block.

4 Make 100 blocks.

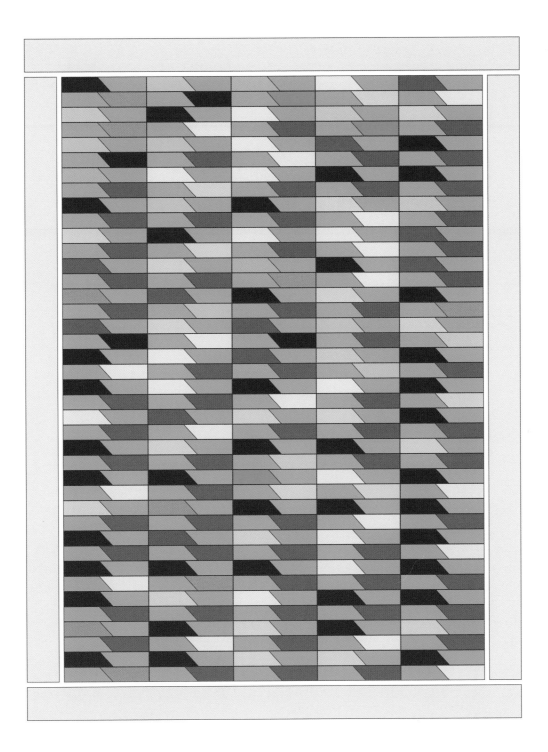

For the tutorial and everything
you need to make this quilt visit:
**www.msqc.co/blocksummer17**

# dizzy
# daisy

*When I was a teenager, roller skating was all the rage. On a typical night out with my gal pals, we'd head to the nearest rink to get our groove on. This story comes from one of my fabulous friends, Cindy. She's always been a whiz on roller skates and I'm sure she can still skate backward to this very day.*

One magical time at the roller rink, I was feeling especially ambitious. I told myself that I would learn how to skate backward that very night. I had just turned sixteen and it was one of my major goals that year—along with learning how to drive and getting the lead in the school play. The mood was right, my striped knee socks fit like a glove, and my skates were freshly oiled up and smoother than ever.

For once, I sat and watched for a few minutes, taking in the atmosphere and gazing wistfully at a long-legged skater who zipped in between and around everyone on the rink with absolute confidence. His blonde, feathered hair floated

## dizzy daisy quilt

in the breeze. To me, he looked like an angel, despite wearing an old baseball t-shirt and tattered jeans. Without realizing what I was doing, I kept staring right at him, and he took notice. He glided up beside me and stopped on a dime without a sound.

At that moment, a slow song came on and he asked me to couple skate with him. I jerked my head up, turning beet red, and nodded yes. He effortlessly engaged me in small talk while I stammered, but pretty soon I confessed my desire to learn how to skate backward. He gave me a grin and pulled me into the middle of the rink to show me how it's done.

With his gentle coaxing, I nervously turned around, glancing over my shoulder to avoid collisions as I took my first few strides backward. It was slow going at first, but with such a charming coach, I improved quickly. The time flew by as I learned to speed up and, sooner than I would have liked, I was back at the railing, watching him skate off again.

My girlfriends immediately mobbed me and asked what happened. I was in a daze and could hardly talk, but we all giggled endlessly about my skating angel for the rest of the night. Even though it's been a while since I last laced up my skates, I'll always fondly remember my days as a dancing queen.

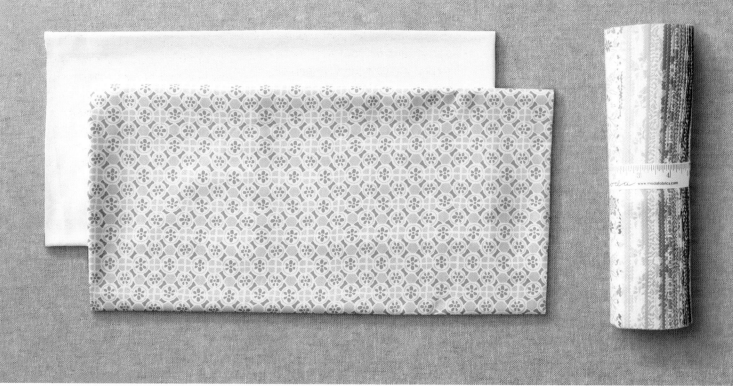

# materials

**QUILT SIZE**
79" X 90"

**BLOCK SIZE**
9" finished

**QUILT TOP**
1 package 10" print squares **or**
  4 matching packages of 5" print
  squares
4¼ yards background fabric –
  includes inner border

**OUTER BORDER**
1¾ yards - includes cornerstones

**BINDING**
¾ yard

**BACKING**
7½ yards - vertical seam(s)

**SAMPLE QUILT**
**Early Bird** by Kate Spain for Moda
Fabrics

# 1 cut

From the background fabric, cut:
- (58) 2½" strips across the
  width of the fabric. Subcut 32
  strips into 2½" squares for
  a **total of 504.** Subcut 18 strips
  into 2½" x 9½" rectangles for a
  **total of 71".** Set aside for
  sashing. Set the remaining strips
  aside for the inner border.

From the outer border fabric, cut:
- (2) 2½" strips across the width
  of the fabric – subcut the
  strips into 2½" squares. Each
  strip will yield 16 squares. A
  **total of 30** squares are needed.
  Set the squares aside to use as
  cornerstones in the sashing. Set
  aside the remainder of the fabric
  for the outer border.

2A

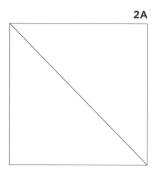

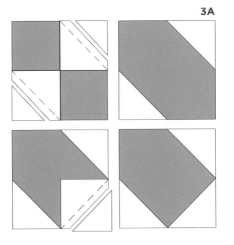

3A

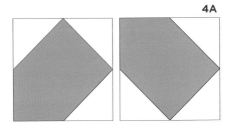

4A

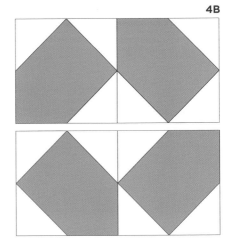

4B

From the package of 10" print squares, cut:
- (4) 5" squares from each for a **total of 168 squares.** Keep all matching prints together.

## 2 mark

On the reverse side of the 2½" background squares, draw a line or press a crease from corner to corner once on the diagonal to mark a sewing line. **2A**

## 3 snowball corners

Place a marked 2½" background square on 2 opposite corners of a 5" square with right sides facing. Sew on the marked sewing line. Trim the excess fabric away ¼" from the sewn seam and press. Place another 2½" marked background square on 1 of the remaining corners and sew on the marked line. Trim the excess fabric away ¼" from the sewn seam and press. Keep all matching prints together. **Make 168 units.** **3A**

## 4 block construction

Sew 2 rows of 2 matching print units together as shown. Notice how each unit is positioned. **4A**

Sew the 2 rows together to complete the block. **Make 42.** **4B**

**Block Size:** 9" finished

## 5 arrange and sew

Lay out the blocks in **7 rows** with each row having **6 blocks.** Place a sashing rectangle between each block. When you are satisfied with the layout, sew the blocks and sashing rectangles together to make a row. Press all seam allowances toward the sashing rectangles. **5A**

## 6 make sashing strips

Sew a sashing rectangle to a print 2½" square (cornerstone). Add another sashing rectangle, then another cornerstone. Continue on in this manner until you have sewn a strip containing 6 sashing rectangles and 5 cornerstones. Press all seam allowances toward the sashing rectangles. **Make 6 sashing strips.** **6A**

Sew the rows together, adding a sashing strip between each row.

## 7 inner border

Sew the remaining (8) 2½" background strips together end-to-end to make one long strip. Trim the borders from this strip. Refer to Borders (pg. 103) in the Construction Basics to measure and cut the inner borders. The strips are approximately 75½" for the sides and approximately 68½" for the top and bottom.

5A

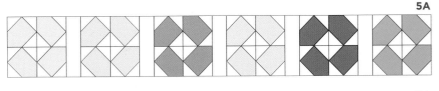

6A

1 On the reverse side of each of the 2½″ background squares, draw a line from corner to corner once on the diagonal or press a crease in place to mark a sewing line.

2 Place a marked 2½″ background square on 2 opposite corners of a 5″ square with right sides facing. Sew on the marked line then trim ¼″ away from the sewn seams.

3 Place another 2½″ marked square on 1 of the remaining corners and sew on the marked line. Trim the excess fabric away ¼″ from the sewn seam and press. This makes 1 quadrant of the block. Make 4.

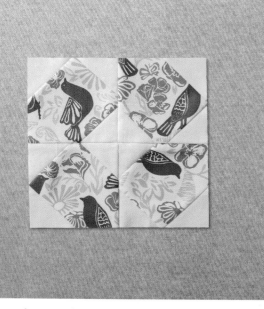

4 Sew 2 rows of 2 quadrants together. Notice how each quadrant is positioned. Sew the 2 rows together to complete 1 block. Make 42.

5 Lay out the blocks in rows with a sashing rectangle between each block. Make sashing strips by sewing a sashing rectangle to a 2½″ cornerstone. Continue in this manner until you have sewn a strip made up of 6 sashing rectangles and 5 cornerstones.

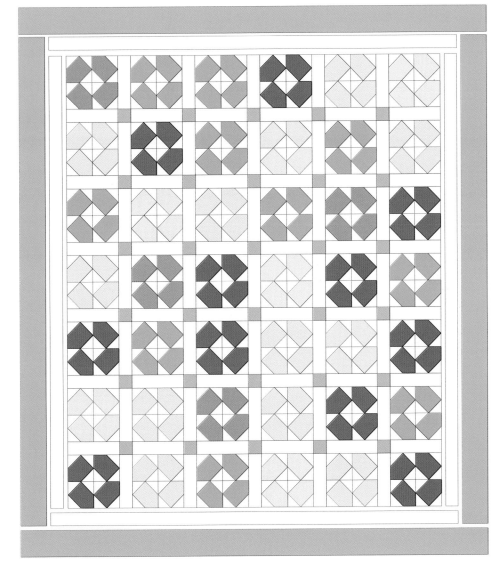

## 8 outer border

Cut (8) 6″ strips across the width of the fabric. Sew the strips together end-to-end to make one long strip. Trim the borders from this strip.

Refer to Borders (pg. 103) in the Construction Basics to measure and cut the outer borders. The strips are approximately 79½″ for the sides and approximately 79½″ for the top and bottom.

## 9 quilt and bind

Layer the quilt with batting and backing and quilt. After the quilting is complete, square up the quilt and trim away all excess batting and backing. Add binding to complete the quilt. See Construction Basics (pg. 103) for binding instructions.

# *emerald*
## *isle*

There was a time, not too many generations ago, when children played outside from dawn till dusk. Free time was filled with homemade fun: backyard expeditions, tadpole hunts, and neighborhood games of kick the can. Kids climbed trees and watched the sun drop slowly until it disappeared below the horizon. They slept out under the stars and felt a closeness to the world around them. In those days, it was easy to find time to daydream and soak in the stillness of quiet moments.

Yes, childhood was simpler in "the good old days." In contrast, kids today are faced with endless distractions and noise. From the moment they wake up to the moment they close their eyes at night, there are a million things competing for attention. Television, video games, and smartphones beg to be noticed; it's not uncommon to see entire groups of young people with their faces glued to tiny, glowing screens.

I chatted with one young mom who resolved to free her children from the unrelenting grasp of electronics for an entire summer. Evelyn started by crafting a daily schedule, and first on the agenda was a technology free-for-all.

Every morning before nine o'clock, the kids were welcome to as much "screen time" as they wanted. However, the

For the tutorial and everything
you need to make this quilt visit:
**www.msqc.co/blocksummer17**

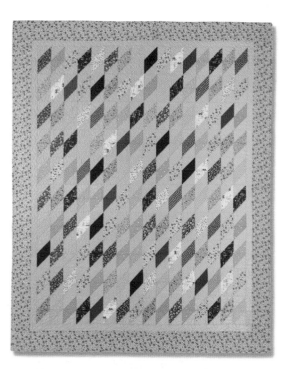

moment the clock struck nine, the screens were shut off. The children were then required to complete a list of activities before they were allowed to return to their electronics.

"You can earn more screen time," Evelyn explained, "by doing something to make our house nice, something to make your body strong, something creative, and something kind."

She provided the children with a long list of ideas: Vacuum the stairs. Jump on the trampoline. Mold a zoo full of animals out of clay. Write a letter to Grandma.

After the kids had completed an activity from each of the four categories, they were allowed twenty minutes of video games or cartoons. But something magical happened as those kids worked for their screen time. Lego cities sprawled across the dining room table, sidewalk chalk masterpieces filled the driveway, new skateboard skills were mastered, and homemade popsicles were shared with elderly neighbors.

Evelyn watched quietly as the children played, learned, and explored far beyond the required amount. Time and time again, screens were forgotten and left behind for happy moments in the sunshine.

It seems that children today are the same as they ever were. They still crave muddy puddles and lightning-fast bike races and ice cream cones that melt so quickly they drip down your elbows. Technology can enrich our lives in many ways, but there's just nothing like a childhood summer filled with real-life adventure.

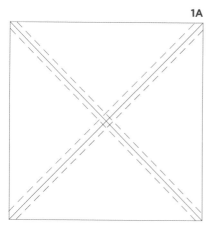

# materials

**QUILT SIZE**
79" X 95"

**BLOCK SIZE**
4" x 8" finished

**QUILT TOP**
1 package 10" print squares
1 package 10" background squares

**INNER BORDER**
¾ yard

**OUTER BORDER**
1¾ yards

**BINDING**
¾ yard

**BACKING**
3 yards - 90" wide

**SAMPLE QUILT**
**Bon Voyage** by My KT for Windham Fabrics

## 1 mark, layer and sew

On the reverse side of each background square, draw a line from corner to corner twice on the diagonal. Place a marked background square atop a print square with right sides facing. Sew ¼" on either side of both diagonal lines. **1A**

Cut the sewn squares through the center vertically and horizontally. Then cut on the marked lines to make 8 half-square triangles. Open and press the seam allowances toward the darker fabric. Square up each half-square triangle to

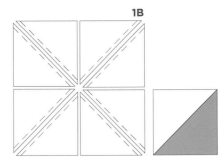

**1B**

4½". Stack the matching half-square triangles together as you cut and press. You will have a **total of 320** half-square triangles. **1B**

## 2 block construction

Pick up 2 matching half-square triangles. Sew them together as shown to complete one block. **Make 160.** **2A**

**Block Size:** 4" x 8" finished

**2A**

## 3 arrange and sew

Lay out the blocks in rows of 16. **Make 10 rows.** Sew the blocks into rows. Press the odd rows toward the left and the even rows toward the right to make the seams "nest." Sew the rows together to complete the center of the quilt.

## 4 inner border

Cut (8) 2½" strips across the width of the fabric. Sew the strips together end-to-end to make one long strip. Trim the borders from this strip.

Refer to Borders (pg. 103) in the Construction Basics to measure and cut the inner borders. The strips are approximately 80½" for the sides and approximately 68½" for the top and bottom.

## 5 outer border

Cut (9) 6" strips across the width of the fabric. Sew the strips together end-to-end to make one long strip. Trim the borders from this strip.

Refer to Borders (pg. 103) in the Construction Basics to measure and cut the outer borders. The strips are approximately 84½" for the sides and approximately 79½" for the top and bottom.

## 6 quilt and bind

Layer the quilt with batting and backing and quilt. After the quilting is complete, square up the quilt and trim away all excess batting and backing. Add binding to complete the quilt. See Construction Basics (pg. 103) for binding instructions.

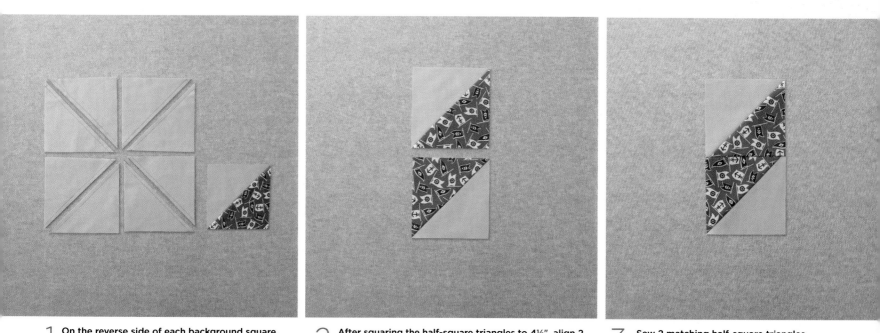

1 On the reverse side of each background square, draw a line from corner to corner twice on the diagonal. Sew ¼" on either side of both diagonal lines. Cut the sewn squares through the center horizontally and vertically, then cut on the drawn lines. Open each unit and press the seam allowance toward the darker fabric.

2 After squaring the half-square triangles to 4½", align 2 matching half-square triangles together as shown.

3 Sew 2 matching half-square triangles together to complete 1 block. Make 160.

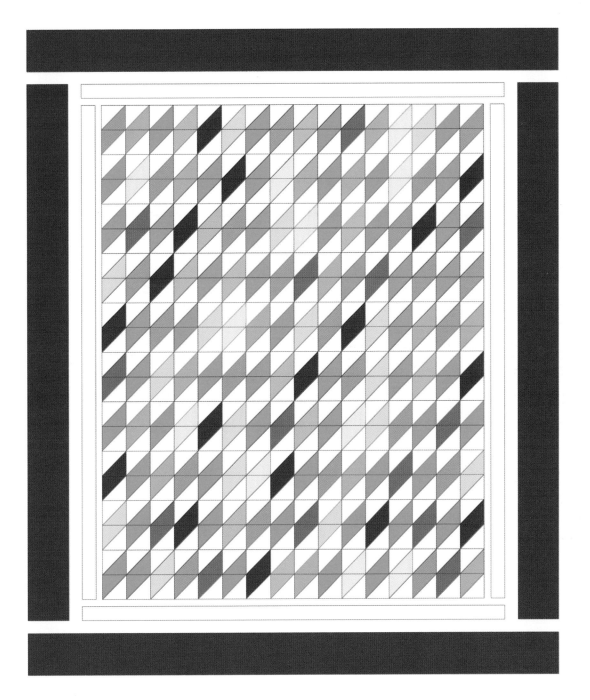

# kindred
## pinwheel

When I was a kid, we rode in the back of pickup trucks; no
one talked about seatbelts and carseats. We played outside
all day, never giving a thought to stranger danger. Our
mothers never knew where we were, they just expected
us home for dinner. In those days, kids could spend an
entire afternoon at the pool without a drop of sunscreen.
We didn't worry about UV rays or things like that. Sunburns
were shrugged off as the first step to a fashionable
golden tan.

As times have changed, there are more and more unwritten
rules parents must follow to feel they are raising their kids
right. Dangers seem much more prevalent, and it takes
dedication to keep those kiddos safe and cared for.

I know a young mother who spends a small fortune on
sunscreen for her four fair-skinned children. Grace had
always been attracted to tall, dark, and handsome men, but
when she grew up, she fell in love and married the palest
man she'd ever met! Spencer was thoughtful and romantic,
and what he lacked in melanin, he made up for in goodness.

For the tutorial and everything you need to make this quilt visit:
**www.msqc.co/blocksummer17**

Soon, the first baby came, a blue-eyed blonde with fair skin. The second baby was as blonde as the first, but with rosy skin. The third and the fourth were no different. These four little munchkins were just as pale as their daddy. They were adorable kids, but after a few minutes in the sun, their sensitive skin would start to fry!

Grace read articles about childhood sunburns and skin cancer, and it terrified her. It was a difficult task, but she was determined to do her best to keep those babies sunburn-free. She stitched up a massive tote bag and filled it with sunscreen lotion, sunscreen spray, hats, sunglasses, and swimsuit covers with SPF.

But just because you fear the sun doesn't mean you have to hide indoors. This cute family loves to play outside. They hike, they swim, and they spend time at the park just about every day. But every outdoor adventure begins with sunscreen. Always sunscreen. Even an impromptu dash through the sprinklers has to wait until everyone is slathered and safe.

Thinking about Grace and her sunscreen vigilance, I look back on the old days with a mixture of longing and shock. In so many ways it was easier, but sometimes I wonder how we all survived! But we did survive, thank goodness, and now it's up to future generations to remember to pack the sunscreen!

# materials

**QUILT SIZE**
91" x 104"

**BLOCK SIZE**
11" finished

**QUILT TOP**
1 package 10" print squares
3¾ yards background fabric
2½ yards dark solid – sashing
½ yard medium solid – cornerstones

**BORDER**
1¾ yards

**BINDING**
1 yard

**BACKING**
8½ yards - horizonal seam(s)

**OTHER SUPPLIES**
Bloc_Loc ruler - optional

**SAMPLE QUILT**
**Sand In My Shoes** by McKenna Ryan
for Robert Kaufman

# 1 cut

Cut each 10" print square in half vertically and horizontally to **make 5" squares.** Each 10" square will yield (4) 5" squares. Cut each square from corner to corner once on the diagonal for a **total of 336** print triangles.

From the background fabric, cut:

- (11) 5" strips across the width of the fabric – subcut each strip into 5" squares. Each strip will yield 8 squares for a **total of 84** squares. Cut each square from corner to corner once on the diagonal to make a **total of 168** triangles.
- (34) 2¼" strips across the width of the fabric – subcut each strip

into 2¼" x 7" rectangles. Each strip will yield 5 rectangles for a **total of 168.**

From the dark solid sashing fabric, cut:

- (33) 2½" strips across the width of the fabric – subcut the strips into 2½" x 11½" rectangles. Each strip will yield 3 rectangles for a **total of 97.**

From the medium solid fabric (cornerstones), cut:

- (4) 2½" strips across the width of the fabric – subcut the strips into 2½" squares. Each strip will yield 16 squares for a **total of 56.**

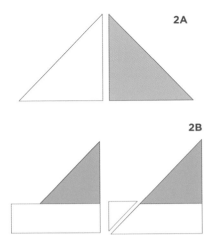

**2A**

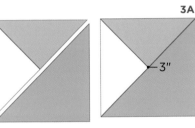

**2B**

**3A**

←3"

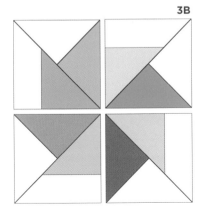

**3B**

# 2 sew

**Unit A** - Pair a print triangle with a background triangle and sew the two together along the outside edge of each as shown.

🐦 **NOTE:** *Be sure the background triangle is always on the left and the print triangle is always on the right.* **Make 168.** 2A

**Unit B** - Align one end of a 2¼" x 7" rectangle with one straight edge of a print triangle and sew the 2 together with right sides facing. Notice the end of the triangle does not extend to the length of the strip. After the rectangle has been sewn in place, align a ruler with the long edge of the triangle and trim the excess fabric from the end of the rectangle. **Make 168.** 2B

# 3 block construction

Sew Unit A to Unit B along the diagonal edge. Press. Align the 45-degree angle on the ruler being used for squaring along the center seam line. Square the unit to 6". This completes one quadrant of the block. **Make 4.**

Sew the 4 quadrants together to complete the block. **Make 42.** 3B

**Block Size:** 11" finished

🐦 **NOTE:** *When squaring the unit to 6", place the 3" mark of the ruler exactly on the point where the (2) 5" triangles that make up Unit A join Unit B. Trim on all 4 sides of the unit.* 3A

# 4 arrange and sew

Lay out the blocks in **7 rows** with each row having **6 blocks**. Place a sashing rectangle between each block and at both ends of each row. When satisfied with the layout, sew the blocks and sashing rectangles together to make a row. Press all seam allowances toward the sashing rectangles. 4A

# 5 make sashing strips

Sew a solid 2½" square (cornerstone) to a sashing rectangle. Add another cornerstone, then a sashing rectangle. Continue on in this manner until you have sewn a strip containing 6 sashing rectangles and 7 cornerstones. Press all seam allowances toward the sashing rectangles. **Make 8** sashing strips. 5A

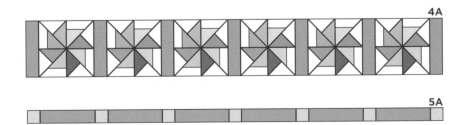

**4A**

**5A**

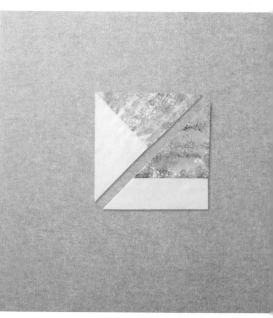

1 Pair a print triangle with a background triangle and sew the two together as shown. The print triangle will always be on the right.

2 Sew a 2¼" x 7" background rectangle to a print triangle. Align a ruler with the long edge of the triangle and trim the excess fabric away from the end of the rectangle.

3 Sew the 2 units together along the diagonal edge to make one quadrant of the block. Make 4.

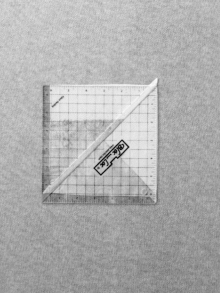

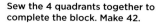

4 Square up each quadrant to 6" after aligning the 3" mark of the ruler exactly at the point where the (2) 5" triangles that make up Unit A join Unit B.

5 After each quadrant is trimmed, press.

6 Sew the 4 quadrants together to complete the block. Make 42.

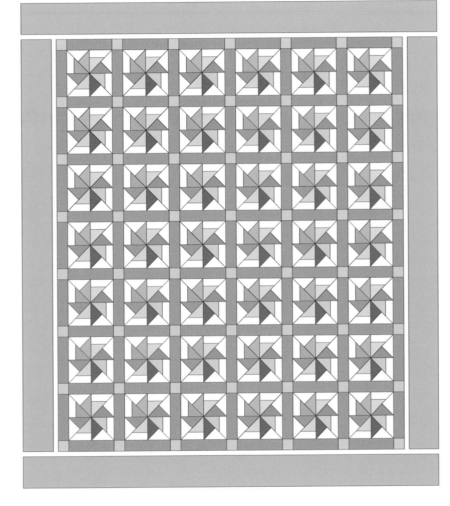

Sew the rows together adding a sashing strip between each row. Add a sashing strip to the top and the bottom as well.

## 6 border

Cut (10) 6" strips across the width of the fabric. Sew the strips together end-to-end to make one long strip. Trim the borders from this strip.

Refer to Borders (pg. 103) in the Construction Basics to measure and cut the outer borders. The strips are approximately 93½" for the sides and approximately 91½" for the top and bottom.

## 7 quilt and bind

Layer the quilt with batting and backing and quilt. After the quilting is complete, square up the quilt and trim away all excess batting and backing. Add binding to complete the quilt. See Construction Basics (pg. 103) for binding instructions.

*For the tutorial and everything you need to make this quilt visit:*

**www.msqc.co/blocksummer17**

# ribbon
## dance

Learning to swim is a rite of passage for a child. That moment when you graduate from water wings to become a full participant in games of Marco Polo and underwater tea party is pure freedom! For kids like Jane, however, that moment never came.

The trouble started when Jane was five years old. She and her two older brothers were playing at a little swimming hole known to the locals as "The Head of the Creek." It was the perfect spot for kids of all ages, with shallow areas for wading as well as deeper pools for more experienced swimmers. Jane was content to explore in knee-deep water, gathering pretty rocks and watching dragonflies flit along the surface of the water.

Without warning, Jane's brothers snuck up, grabbed her by the wrists and ankles, and tossed her into the deep. She sunk like a rock, eyes wide open. After what seemed like an eternity, the boys jumped in and pulled her out, laughing.

"Sorry! We thought you'd at least float. Everyone floats." Jane didn't float. And from that moment on, she carried with her a terrible fear of deep water.

When Jane was seven years old, the city built a brand new wave pool and it quickly became the place to be. While her friends lined up to try out the new high dive, Jane kept to the shallow end with the preschool crowd. She wasn't even jealous. She just accepted the fact that she was never going to swim.

When she was sixteen, Jane spent the day at a waterpark with her friends. She was more than willing to ride the waterslides that emptied into shallow water, but the ones that landed in deep pools were out of the question. But as her friends trotted off to try the new triple-death-defying slide, the new boy, Jason, stayed behind. Jason was tall with dark brown hair and a deep, golden tan. And, as luck would have it, he was also a lifeguard with a letter from the high school swim team.

"I'm going to teach you how to swim." Jason announced, and that was that. After a few early morning sessions at the pool with her own private swim coach, Jane was swimming. She never got very fast, but at least she wasn't stuck in the kiddie pool any longer! I guess it's easier to face your fears when a cute boy in swim trunks offers to hold your hand the entire time!

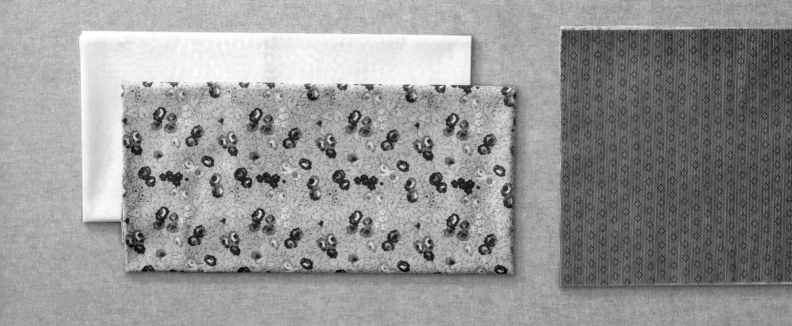

# materials

**QUILT SIZE**
78″ X 86″

**BLOCK SIZE**
8″ x 12″ finished

**QUILT TOP**
1 package 10″ print squares
1 package 10″ background squares

**INNER BORDER**
¾ yard

**OUTER BORDER**
1½ yards

**BINDING**
¾ yard

**BACKING**
7¼ yards - horizontal seam(s)

**SAMPLE QUILT**
**Linen and Lawn** by Sue Daley for
Riley Blake Designs

# 1 make half-square triangles

Draw a line from corner to corner twice on the diagonal on the reverse side of the background squares.

Select 36 print squares. Layer a background square with a print square with right sides facing and sew on both sides of each drawn line using a ¼″ seam allowance. Cut the sewn squares in half vertically and horizontally, then on the drawn lines. Open and press each seam allowance toward the darker fabric. Each pair of sewn squares will yield 8 half-square triangles for

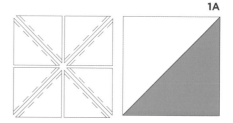

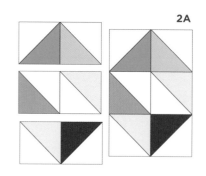

a **total of 288.** Square each half-square triangle unit to 4½". **1A**

## 2 block construction

Each block consists of 6 assorted half-square triangle units. Sew the units together into rows of 2. **Make 3 rows** as shown and sew the rows together to complete the block. **Make 48.** **2A**

**Block Size:** 8" x 12" finished

## 3 arrange in rows

Lay out the blocks in **rows of 8.** Sew the blocks together to complete a row. **Make 6 rows.** Press the seam allowances in the even-numbered rows toward the right and the odd-numbered rows toward the left. This will make the seams nest together at the corners.

After the rows have been pressed, sew them together to complete the center of the quilt.

## 4 inner border

Cut (8) 2½" strips across the width of the fabric. Sew the strips together end-to-end to make one long strip. Trim the borders from this strip.

Refer to Borders (pg. 103) in the Construction Basics to measure and cut the inner borders. The strips are approximately 72½" for the sides and approximately 68½" for the top and bottom.

## 5 outer border

Cut (8) 5½" strips across the width of the fabric. Sew the strips together end-to-end to make one long strip. Trim the borders from this strip.

Refer to Borders (pg. 103) in the Construction Basics to measure and cut the outer borders. The strips are approximately 76½" for the sides and approximately 78½" for the top and bottom.

## 6 quilt and bind

Layer the quilt with batting and backing and quilt. After the quilting is complete, square up the quilt and trim away all excess batting and backing. Add binding to complete the quilt. See Construction Basics (pg. 103) for binding instructions.

# Bonus Project: Ribbon Dance Table Runner

**RUNNER SIZE**
19" x 39"

**BLOCK SIZE**
8" x 12" finished

**RUNNER TOP**
(3) 10" print squares
(3) 10" background squares

**BORDER**
½ yard

**BINDING**
½ yard

**BACKING**
1 yard

## 1 make half-square triangles

Draw a line from corner to corner twice on the diagonal on the reverse side of 3 background squares. Select 3 print squares. Layer a background square with a print square with right sides facing and sew on both sides of each drawn line using a ¼" seam allowance. Cut the sewn squares in half vertically and horizontally, then on the drawn lines. Open and press each seam allowance toward the darker fabric. Each pair of sewn squares will yield 8 half-square triangles for a **total of 24.** Square each half-square triangle unit to 4½". **1A**

## 2 block construction

Each block consists of 6 assorted half-square triangle units. Sew the units together into rows of 2. **Make 3 rows** as shown and sew the rows together to complete the block. **Make 4.** **2A**

Sew the 4 blocks together into a strip.

## 3 border

Cut (3) 4" strips across the width of the fabric. Sew the strips together end-to-end to make one long strip. Trim the borders from this strip.

Refer to Borders (pg. 103) in the Construction Basics to measure and cut the borders. The strips are approximately 32½" for the top and bottom and approximately 19½" for the ends.

## 4 quilt and bind

Layer the table runner with batting and backing and quilt. After the quilting is complete, square up the edges and trim away all excess batting and backing. Add binding to complete the table runner. See Construction Basics (pg. 103) for binding instructions.

1 On the reverse side of each 10″ background square, draw a line from corner to corner twice on the diagonal. Layer the background square with a print square with right sides facing. Sew on both sides of each line using a ¼″ seam allowance.

2 Cut the sewn squares in half vertically and horizontally, then cut on the drawn lines. Open each to reveal a half-square triangle unit.

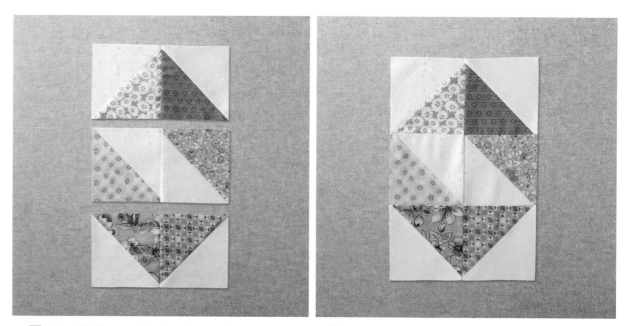

3 Sew 2 half-square triangle units together as shown to make each of 3 rows.

4 Sew the rows together to complete the block. Make 48.

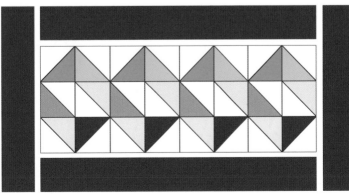

# small dashing stars

Great-Grandma didn't know what she was in for that Fourth of July. It was a humid day and we were all feeling laid-back. The hot dogs sizzled on the grill. Popsicles melted in the children's hands, leaving sticky red and blue rivulets running down their arms. A dozen woven plaid lawn chairs were set up around the edge of a kiddie pool and we all had our feet marinating in the lukewarm water. The familiar scene was comforting, like a bowl of potato salad. As we relaxed in the hot July sunshine, we savored the carefree spirit of the day.

The day turned to dusk and a cool breeze began to blow. Clouds gathered on the horizon. Sensing a change in the weather, the kids raced about with renewed enthusiasm and started begging for the fireworks show to begin already! In the middle of Missouri, just about anything goes, and we tend to cause a ruckus that leaves dogs howling in a mile radius.

It all began innocently enough. Each child received one sparkler and as many pop-its as they could handle. Then, we got out the whistling Petes. The kids excitedly plugged their

*For the tutorial and everything you need to make this quilt visit:* **www.msqc.co/blocksummer17**

ears as we lit off a few. After that came a parade of fountains, pinwheels, ground bloom flowers, bottle rockets, and those little charcoal snakes that grow.

Finally, we got out the big guns. Sky rockets, or mortars, aren't technically allowed, but owing to the fact that we have kind neighbors, we had picked up a few dozen for the grand finale. The children went back indoors to watch with bated breath through the large picture window and the adults all lined up on the edge of the lawn. Great-Grandma sat at the end, looking on contentedly. It was her ninety-fifth time celebrating the Fourth of July, after all.

With a great BOOM, the mortars exploded one by one in the twilight. Sparks showered down, grazing the treetops. But before the next mortar was launched into the sky, the cardboard tube toppled over and it shot directly toward the lawn chairs. We all jumped out of our seats and raced toward the house before the mortar could explode, but in our haste we'd abandoned Great-Grandma! She sat there dazed as a hailstorm of sparks rained down all around her.

Luckily, our dear great-grandmother was unscathed. She came out of it a little confused, and maybe temporarily deafened a bit, but she laughed it off, shaking her bony finger at us. Later on she told us that it was the most fun she'd had in some time. We hope you all have a wonderful Fourth of July and let's be sure to keep all those grandmas safe out there!

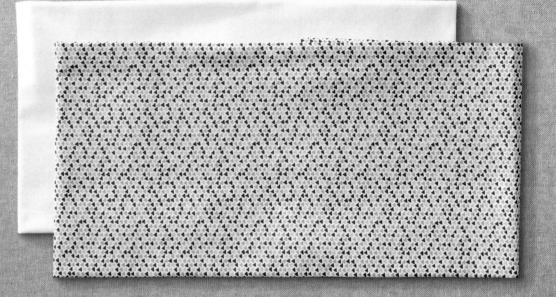

# materials

**QUILT SIZE**
56½" X 56½"

**BLOCK SIZE**
10½" finished

**QUILT TOP**
2 matching packages 5" print squares
2 yards background fabric

**BORDER**
1¼ yards – includes squares used in blocks and cornerstones

**BINDING**
¾ yard

**BACKING**
3¾ yards - vertical seam(s)

**SAMPLE QUILT**
**Sunday Supper** by Sweetwater for Moda Fabrics

# 1 cut

From the background fabric, cut:

- (4) 5" strips across the width of the fabric – subcut each strip into (8) 5" squares for a **total of 32.**
- (6) 3⅛" strips across the width of the fabric – subcut each strip into (12) 3⅛" squares for a **total of 64.**
- (14) 2" strips across the width of the fabric – subcut each strip into (3) 2" x 11" rectangles for a **total of 40**. Set the strips aside to use as sashing rectangles.

From the border fabric, cut:

- (5) 2" strips across the width of the fabric – subcut each strip into (20) 2" squares for a **total of 89.** There will be a few squares left over. Set aside the remainder of the fabric for the border.

# 2 block construction

Select 1 pair of light matching 5" print squares and one pair of contrasting 5" print squares.

Place a 5" background square atop a light 5" print square with right sides

**2A**

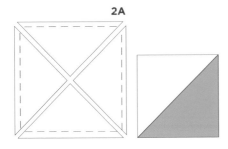

**2B**

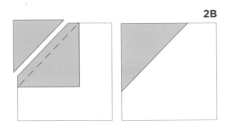

**2C**

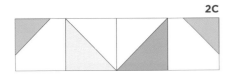

**2D**

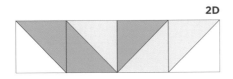

**2E**

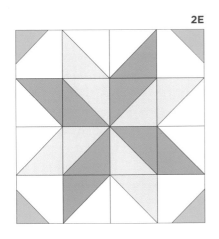

facing. Sew around the perimeter of the square ¼" from the edge. Cut the stitched square from corner to corner twice on the diagonal. Open to reveal 4 matching half-square triangles. Press the seam allowance toward the darker fabric. **2A**

In the same manner, **make 4** matching half-square triangles using a 5" background square and a contrasting 5" print square.

Place the remaining (2) 5" print squares together with right sides facing. **Make 4** matching half-square triangles in the same manner as before. Square each of the half-square triangles to 3⅛".

**Mark (4) 2" squares** from corner to corner once on the diagonal on the reverse side. Place a marked square on one corner of a 3⅛" background square with right sides facing. Sew on the marked line. Trim the excess fabric away ¼" from the stitched seam. We'll call these corner units for the sake of clarity. **Make 4** for each block. **2B**

Sew a corner unit to a light/background half-square triangle unit. Add a dark/background half-square triangle unit then another corner unit. **Make 2 rows** like this. **2C**

Sew a dark/background half-square triangle unit to a dark/light half-square triangle unit. Add another dark/light half-square triangle unit then a light/background half-square triangle unit. **Make 2 rows** like this. **2D**

Sew the 4 rows together to complete the block. **Make 16 blocks.** **2E**

**Block Size:** 10½" finished

# 3 lay out blocks and sashing

Lay out the blocks in **4 rows** with each row having **4 blocks**. Sew the rows together, adding a sashing rectangle between each block and at each end. Press the seam allowances toward the blocks. **3A**

**3A**

**3B**

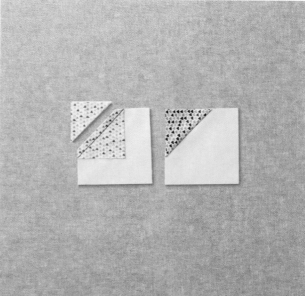

1  Place a 5″ background square atop a light 5″ print square with right sides facing. Sew around the perimeter of the square ¼″ from the edge. Cut the stitched square from corner to corner twice on the diagonal. Open to reveal 4 matching half-square triangles.

2  Mark (4) 2″ squares from corner to corner once on the diagonal. Place a marked square on one corner of a 3⅛″ background square and sew on the marked line. Trim the excess fabric away ¼″ from the sewn seam.

3  Sew corner units and half-square triangles together as shown to make the top and bottom rows. Sew half-square triangles together as shown to make the 2 center rows of the block.

4  Sew the 4 rows together to complete the block. Make 16.

Make a sashing strip by sewing a 2″ x 11″ sashing rectangle to a 2″ print square cut from the border fabric. Add another sashing rectangle and another print 2″ square. Continue in this manner until you have a strip consisting of 5 squares and 4 rectangles. End the strip with a 2″ square. Press all seam allowances toward the 2″ print squares. **Make 5** and sew them between each row as well as to the top and bottom of the center of the quilt. **3B**

# 4 border

Cut (6) 4″ strips across the width of the fabric. Sew the strips together end-to-end to make one long strip. Trim the borders from this strip. Refer to Borders (pg. 103) in the Construction Basics to measure and cut the outer borders. The strips are approximately 50″ for the sides and approximately 57″ for the top and bottom.

# 5 quilt and bind

Layer the quilt with batting and backing and quilt. After the quilting is complete, square up the quilt and trim away all excess batting and backing. Add binding to complete the quilt. See Construction Basics (pg. 103) for binding instructions.

# summer
## notes

A quilting friend named Fran was always an A+ mom at the start of the school year. After a slow, relaxing summer, she was totally up for the challenge of organizing her crew as they boarded the bus toward a magical new year of learning and fun.

Every night Fran helped the children select clean, matching outfits for the next day. She even pressed out the wrinkles! Backpacks were loaded with neatly completed homework and beautifully packed lunches. Fran even included little notes of encouragement for the kids to find at lunchtime.

In the morning, Fran would wake the family with plenty of time for a nice breakfast. After they had eaten, they loved to turn up the radio and sing along as Fran combed and braided and curled each little head of hair. Yes, Fran was pretty much supermom. For about a month.

As the novelty of a new school year started to wear off, her superpowers seemed to weaken. Pancakes and scrambled eggs were replaced with cold cereal and last night's mac n' cheese. Homework was sometimes forgotten, and lunches were rarely worthy of a post on social media.

For the tutorial and everything you need to make this quilt visit:
**www.msqc.co/blocksummer17**

By the end of the year, the kids weren't the only ones longing for lazy mornings and late nights on the trampoline. After all, who can focus on spelling tests when the weather is warm and the sun stays up way past bedtime? Those last few weeks were always a real struggle for Fran, so when summer finally arrived, it was cause for celebration! Schedules were tossed out the window and replaced with easy, spontaneous fun.

Summertime was made for children. The slow pace of unhurried days allows young imaginations plenty of room to stretch and grow. Day after day, Fran and the kids ran through sprinklers, blew bubbles, and sipped lemonade on the front porch. Afternoons were spent in the cool of the house, coloring, and reading stories under makeshift blanket forts.

And by the time summer came to an end, after weeks and weeks of perfect simplicity, Fran was always ready for a new year of school, schedules, and early morning stacks of buttery flapjacks.

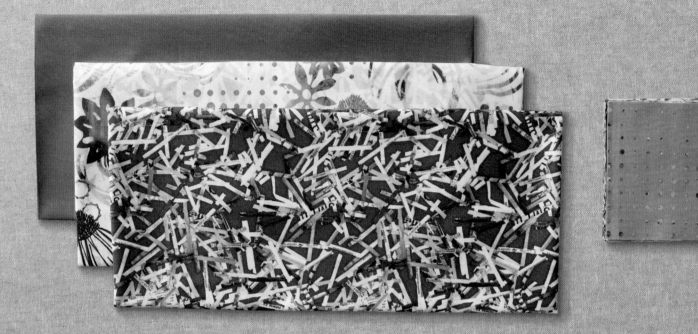

# materials

**QUILT SIZE**
57" X 57"

**BLOCK SIZE**
16" finished

**QUILT TOP**
2 packages 5" print squares
2 packages 5" background squares
**or** 1½ yards

**BORDER**
1 yard

**BINDING**
¾ yard

**BACKING**
3¾ yards - vertical seam(s)

**SAMPLE QUILT**
**Urban Artifacts** by Leslie Tucker
Jenison for RJR Fabric

# 1 cut

If you are using precut 5" background
squares, skip the cutting directions and
follow the directions for making half-
square triangle units.

From the background fabric, cut:

- (9) 5" strips across the width of
  the fabric. Subcut each strip into
  (8) 5" squares for a **total of 72.**

# 2 make half-square triangle units

Draw a line from corner to corner once
on the diagonal on the reverse side of

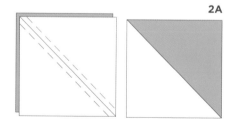

2A

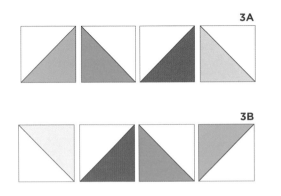

3A

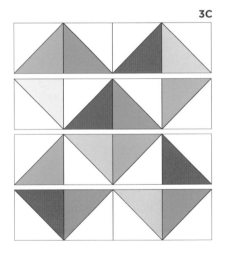

3B

3C

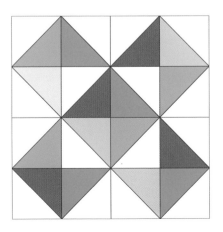

(72) 5″ background squares. Layer a marked background square with a 5″ print square with right sides facing. Sew on both sides of the drawn line, using a ¼″ seam allowance. Cut on the drawn line. Open each unit and press the seam allowance toward the darker fabric. Square each unit to 4½″. Each sewn square yields 2 half-square triangle units and a **total of 144** units are needed. 2A

## 3 block construction

Sew the half-square triangles into 4 rows of 4. Arrange the half-square triangles as shown to make rows 1 and 4. 3A

Arrange the half-square triangles as shown to make rows 2 and 3. 3B

Sew the 4 rows together to complete the block. **Make 9.** 3C

**Block Size:** 16″ finished

## 4 arrange and sew

Arrange the blocks in **3 rows of 3**. Sew the blocks together. Press the seam allowances of rows 1 and 3 toward the right and the center row toward the left to make the seams "nest."

Sew the 3 rows together to complete the center of the quilt.

## 5 border

Cut (6) 5″ strips across the width of the fabric. Sew the strips together end-to-end to make one long strip. Trim the borders from this strip.

Refer to Borders (pg. 103) in the Construction Basics to measure and cut the outer borders. The strips are approximately 48½″ for the sides and approximately 57½″ for the top and bottom.

## 6 quilt and bind

Layer the quilt with batting and backing and quilt. After the quilting is complete, square up the quilt and trim away all excess batting and backing. Add binding to complete the quilt. See Construction Basics (pg. 103) for binding instructions.

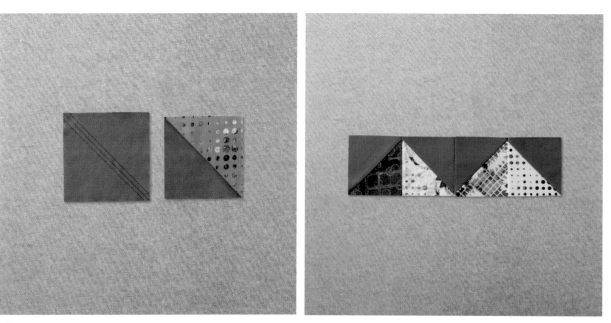

1 Draw a line from corner to corner once on the diagonal of each background 5" square. Layer a background 5" square with a print 5" square and sew on both sides of the line using a ¼" seam allowance. Cut on the drawn line and open to reveal 2 half-square triangle units.

2 Arrange 4 half-square triangles as shown to make rows 1 and 4. Sew the units together. Make 2.

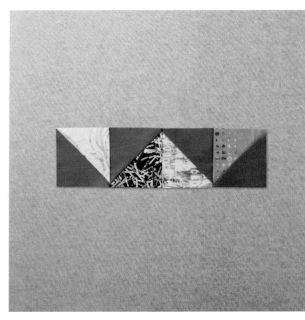

3 Arrange the half-square triangles as shown to make rows 2 and 3.

4 Sew the 4 rows together as shown to complete the block. Make 9.

For the tutorial and everything you need to make this quilt visit:
www.msqc.co/blocksummer17

# tender
## hearts

I can't believe it took me until my fifties to finally visit Hawaii. I had been dreaming of it for years, but it never seemed like a possibility. As a little girl, when the hula was at the height of its popularity, I'd turn on island music and sway my hips to the ukelele with a blanket wrapped around my waist. Then, as a teenager, I was interested in scuba diving and became a certified diver. I'd always dreamed of swimming with tropical fish, but I had to be content with the chilly waters of the Pacific. Later on, as Missouri Star Quilt Company grew, I came to realize that there were quilters all over the world who wanted to learn along with our tutorials and I seized the opportunity to visit the islands. All my childhood dreams were finally coming true!

Within an hour of getting off the plane, I had my toes in the warm ocean. It was the most incredible feeling. I knew it wouldn't be cold, but I had no idea how clear and beautiful the aqua water would be. I saw tiny, glinting fish darting around my legs as I waded out a bit further and then I actually spied a turtle! It bobbed up like a cork and drifted

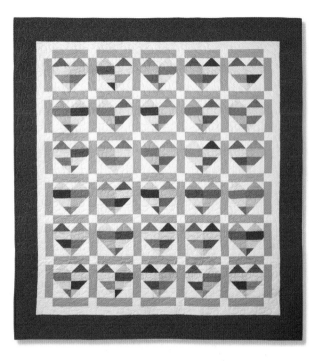

off a ways before it plunged back beneath the surface. I was completely awestruck.

That night Ron and I sat on the beach as the sun went down, watching a dazzling sunset and eating the most delicious dinner, a traditional "plate lunch" with sticky white rice, rich macaroni salad, and pulled pork, along with fresh tropical fruit. I'd never had such sweet mango or pineapple in my life. I could eat that kind of simple, good food every day.

There are so many things about Hawaii that amaze me: the flora and fauna, the laid back attitude, the delicious food, but most of all, I love the people. As I walked into a local quilt shop, the spirit of aloha was tangible. There was so much love in that room! I was also in awe of the talent I saw everywhere I went. Hawaiian quilting has always struck me as impressive, but seeing these talented islanders working at their craft helped me gain a brand new appreciation for their skill. We learned together, laughed together, and parted ways much too soon, feeling like ohana (family).

Recently, I've been back to Hawaii to celebrate the marriage of my son. I couldn't imagine a better place to start a new life together. To me, Hawaii is a magical place filled with fond memories and I anticipate many happy returns.

# materials

**QUILT SIZE**
72″ X 77″

**BLOCK SIZE**
9″ x 8″ finished

**QUILT TOP**
1 roll of 2½″ strips
2½ yards background fabric –
includes inner border and
   cornerstones
1½ yards contrasting solid
 - sashing rectangles

**OUTER BORDER**
1½ yards

**BINDING**
¾ yard

**BACKING**
4¾ yards - vertical seam(s)

**SAMPLE QUILT**
**Kona Cotton Solids Blushing
Bouquet Palette** by RK Studios
for Robert Kaufman

# 1 cut

From the background fabric, cut:
- (8) 5″ strips across the width of the fabric – subcut each strip into (8) 5″ squares for a **total of 60.** There will be 4 squares left over. Cut (2) 2½″ squares from one of the leftovers. Add these to the squares to be set aside for cornerstones. (See next cutting instruction.)
- (17) 2½″ strips across the width of the fabric – subcut 10 strips into (16) 2½″ squares for a **total of 160.** Set the rest of the strips aside for the inner border.

Set 42 squares aside for the cornerstones. (Be sure to include the 2 squares you cut from the leftover 5″ squares.)

From the contrasting solid fabric, cut:
- (18) 2½″ strips across the width of the fabric. Subcut 9 strips into 2½″ x 9½″ rectangles for the horizontal sashing rectangles, for a **total of 35.** Subcut the remaining strips into 2½″ x 8½″ rectangles for the vertical sashing rectangles, for a **total of 36.**

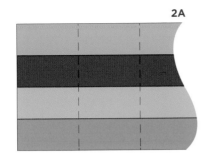

**2A**

## 2 make strip sets

Choose 4 contrasting strips from the roll. Sew the strips together along the long sides. **Make 8** strip sets. Subcut each strip set into (8) 5" x 8½" rectangles. Set the remaining strips aside for another project. **2A**

## 3 block construction

**Snowball Corners** - Fold (4) 2½" background squares once on the diagonal and press the crease in place to mark a sewing line. Place a creased 2½" background square on one corner of a 5" x 8½" strip-pieced rectangle with right sides facing. Stitch on the sewing line, then trim the excess fabric ¼" away from the sewn seam. Repeat for the adjacent side of the rectangle. **Make 2** and sew them together vertically as shown. **3A**

Fold (2) 5" background squares once on the diagonal and press the crease in place to mark a sewing line. Place a creased 5" background square atop one lower corner of the block with right sides facing. Sew on the marked sewing line. Move the piece over ½" from the sewn seam and stitch another seam line. Repeat for the adjacent lower corner of the block. Using your rotary

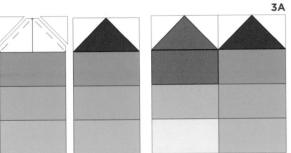

**3A**

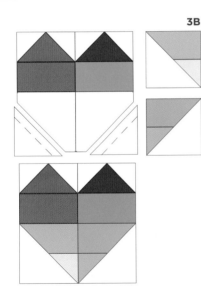

**3B**

cutter, cut between the two sewn seams. Open the corners and press the seam allowances toward the darker fabric. **3B**

**Make 30 blocks.**
**Block Size:** 9" x 8" finished

**NOTE:** *Set the small "bonus" half-square triangles aside for another project. There will be enough to make a table runner, if you choose.*

## 4 arrange and sew

Lay out the blocks in **6 rows of 5**. Add a 2½" x 8½" solid sashing rectangle between each block and at the end of each row as shown. Sew the blocks and rectangles together to complete each row. **4A**

Sew a solid 2½" x 9½" rectangle to a 2½" background square, add a 2½" background square then another 2½" x 9½" rectangle. Continue on in this manner until you have a strip that consists of (6) 2½" background squares and (5) 2½" x 9½" sashing rectangles. **Make 7** sashing strips. **4B**

Sew the rows together, adding a sashing strip between each row. Add a sashing strip to the top and to the bottom to complete the center of the quilt. (See diagram on pg. 79.)

## 5 inner border

Pick up the (7) 2½" background strips you set aside for the inner border. Sew the strips together end-to-end to make one long strip. Trim the borders from this strip.

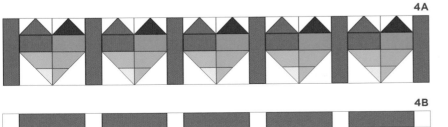

**4A**

**4B**

1   Choose 4 contrasting strips from the roll. Sew the strips together along the long edges. Make 8 strips sets and cut each into (8) 5″ x 8½″ rectangles.

2   Place a marked 2½″ background square on one corner of a strip-pieced rectangle. Sew on the sewing line, then trim the excess fabric away ¼″ from the sewn seam. Repeat for the adjacent corner.

3   Pair 2 snowballed rectangles.

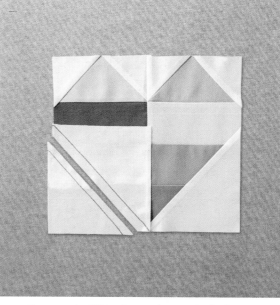

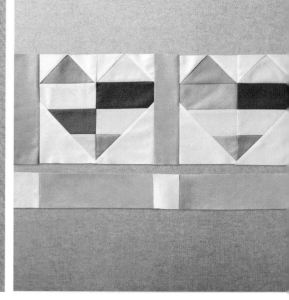

4   Sew the 2 snowballed rectangles together.

5   Sew a marked 5″ background square to the lower corner of the strip-pieced block. Sew on the marked line. Move the piece over ½″ from the sewn seam and stitch another seam. Cut between the two seams. Repeat for the adjacent corner. Save the extra half-square triangles for another project.

6   Sew the blocks together into rows, adding a sashing rectangle between the blocks and on the end of each row. Join the rows with horizontal sashing strips.

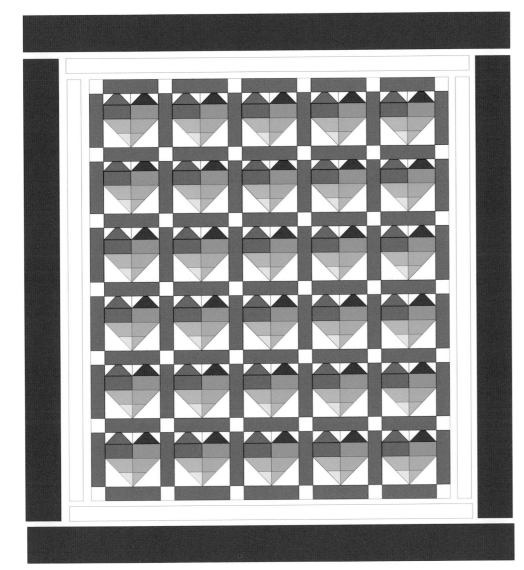

Refer to Borders (pg. 103) in the Construction Basics to measure and cut the inner borders. The strips are approximately 62½" for the sides and approximately 61½" for the top and bottom.

## 6 outer border

Cut (7) 6" strips across the width of the fabric. Sew the strips together end-to-end to make one long strip. Trim the borders from this strip.

Refer to Borders (pg. 103) in the Construction Basics to measure and cut the outer borders. The strips are approximately 66½" for the sides and approximately 72½" for the top and bottom.

## 7 quilt and bind

Layer the quilt with batting and backing and quilt. After the quilting is complete, square up the quilt and trim away all excess batting and backing. Add binding to complete the quilt. See Construction Basics (pg. 9) for binding instructions.

*You'll have extra half-square triangle blocks left over from making this quilt. We turned ours into a cute table runner! See image on pg. 74.*

# under
## *construction*

My mom worked one summer while we were renovating the house. Being twelve, I had been given some new responsibilities to help her out like checking the mail, vacuuming, and putting dinner in the oven. It was kind of exciting, experiencing this newfound maturity. I wanted to show that I could be trusted, so I tried my very best, but sometimes my playful nature got the better of me.

The house had been without a working oven for a few weeks, but finally the new kitchen was put in and it was marvelous. At the time it was absolutely chic, decked out in avocado appliances with shiny chrome trim. I was in awe as I stroked each gleaming surface, imagining myself as a housewife with my very own family, cooking in such a beautiful kitchen.

One fateful day, my mom left me a short note explaining what would be for dinner that night. On the counter next to the note was a large can that read, "English Beef Pie." I skimmed the note and thought, simple enough, turned the

For the tutorial and everything you need to make this quilt visit:
**www.msqc.co/blocksummer17**

oven to 400 degrees, peeled the label off the can, placed it in a baking tin, and set it inside the oven. I dusted my hands off, feeling accomplished, and went into the living room to kick back and watch a little TV. But I had made a critical error.

As the can baked in the oven, the pressure built up inside and it exploded like a bomb. From the living room, I heard something that sounded like a gunshot coming from the kitchen. I jumped off the sofa and rolled onto the floor, worried that I was under attack. Hearing nothing else, I crept into the kitchen to find absolute carnage. The beautiful new oven door had been blown off and the remains of the English Beef Pie was spattered all over the

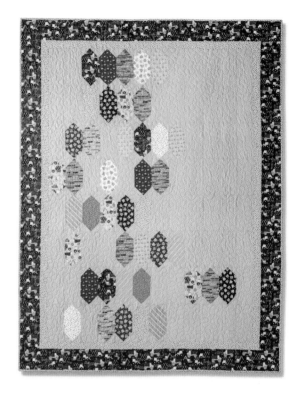

new linoleum floor and sparkling formica countertops. I was dumbfounded. How had this happened?

As I stood amidst the wreckage, unsure of what to do, my mom suddenly walked into the kitchen and gasped. My dad just shook his head, suppressing a laugh, as my mom slowly picked up a sponge and started cleaning it all up. I snapped out of my shock and started wiping the floor. Later on, they kindly reminded me to read all of the instructions on the can and to open it up next time. I wasn't in trouble, but I had definitely learned my lesson! Thankfully, I don't think another can of English Beef Pie ever showed up in our house again.

# materials

**QUILT SIZE**
69" X 91"

**BLOCK SIZE**
4½" x 9½" finished

**QUILT TOP**
1 package 10" print squares
3 yards background fabric

**INNER BORDER**
¾ yard

**OUTER BORDER**
1½ yards

**BINDING**
¾ yard

**BACKING**
5½ yards - vertical seam(s)

**SAMPLE QUILT**
**Big Dig** by Whistler Studios for
Windham Fabrics

## 1 cut

Select (21) 10" print squares from the package. Cut each square in half vertically to make (2) 5" x 10" rectangles for a **total of 42.** Set the rest of the squares aside for another project.

From the background fabric, cut:

- (7) 10" strips across the width of the fabric – subcut each strip into (8) 5" x 10" rectangles for a **total of 56.** There will be 2 rectangles left over for another project

- (12) 2¾" strips across the width of the fabric – Subcut each strip into (14) 2¾" squares for a **total of 168.**

2A

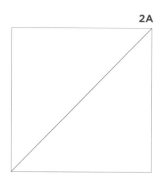

## 2 block construction

On the reverse side of each 2¾"
background square, draw a line from
corner to corner once on the diagonal.
2A

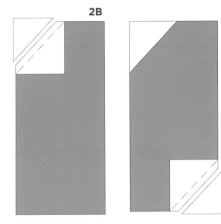

2B

Place a marked background square on
1 corner of a 5" x 10" print rectangle.
Sew on the marked line, then trim ¼"
from the sewn seam. Open, then press the
seam allowance toward the darker fabric.
Repeat for the opposing corner. **2B**

Repeat for the remaining 2 corners of
the rectangle to complete the block.
**Make 42.** 2C

**Block Size:** 4½" x 9½" Finished

2C

## 3 arrange and sew

Arrange the blocks and background
rectangles in rows. Each row is made up
of **12 rectangles/blocks**. See the diagram
on (pg. 87) for placement purposes.
**Make 8 rows**. Press the seam allowances
of the odd rows toward the left and the
even rows toward the right to make the
seams "nest."

After the rows have been pressed, sew
them together to complete the center
of the quilt.

## 4 inner border

Cut (7) 2½" strips across the width of the
fabric. Sew the strips together end-to-end
to make one long strip. Trim the borders
from this strip.

Refer to Borders (pg. 103) in the
Construction Basics to measure and
cut the inner borders. The strips are
approximately 76½" for the sides and
approximately 58½" for the top and
bottom.

## 5 outer border

Cut (8) 6" strips across the width of the
fabric. Sew the strips together end-to-end
to make one long strip. Trim the borders
from this strip.

Refer to Borders (pg. 103) in the
Construction Basics to measure and
cut the outer borders. The strips are
approximately 80½" for the sides and
approximately 69½" for the top and
bottom.

## 6 quilt and bind

Layer the quilt with batting and backing
and quilt. After the quilting is complete,
square up the quilt and trim away all
excess batting and backing. Add binding
to complete the quilt. See Construction
Basics (pg. 103) for binding instructions.

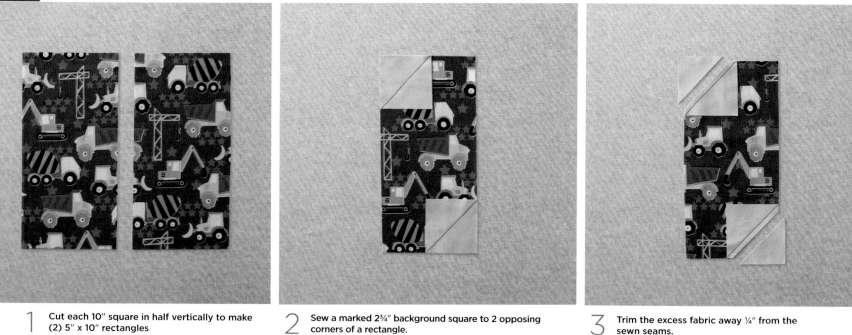

1   Cut each 10″ square in half vertically to make (2) 5″ x 10″ rectangles

2   Sew a marked 2¾″ background square to 2 opposing corners of a rectangle.

3   Trim the excess fabric away ¼″ from the sewn seams.

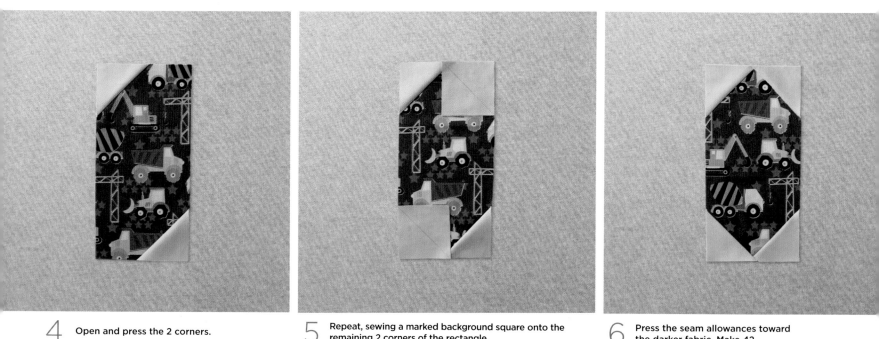

4   Open and press the 2 corners.

5   Repeat, sewing a marked background square onto the remaining 2 corners of the rectangle.

6   Press the seam allowances toward the darker fabric. Make 42.

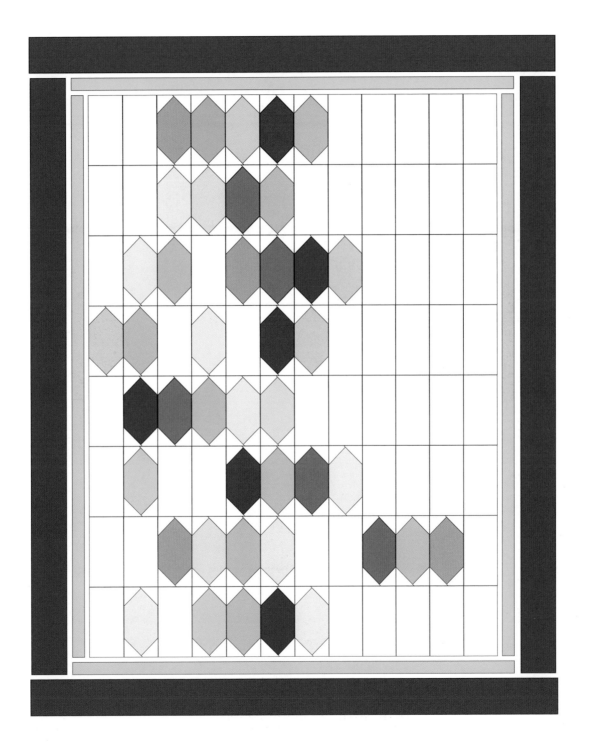

# thread
# talk

*Needle little more thread? Well, don't feel spoolish if you have a few questions. Have you ever stood in the middle of the notions aisle, gazing at rows of thread in a rainbow of colors, wondering where to begin? We all start somewhere and with so many options out there, it can be downright confusing. Should I get cotton or polyester? What's the difference between 40 and 50 weight? Do I need more than one kind of thread? Hold on, we're here to help!*

### A COMMON THREAD

Running through all our beautiful quilts is a common thread. We can't make anything without it! There are many different attitudes about thread. Some grab the nearest spool, regardless of the color, and stitch away without giving a single thought to the weight or the quality, while others own a well-organized library of thread in a rainbow of hues of the highest caliber. Most of us fall somewhere in between. But no matter what kind of thread we choose to use, it's important to recognize that different kinds of threads have varying qualities and will wear differently. Here are a few hints for choosing the right thread to help your project last as long as possible.

## POLYESTER

In the early 1940's, polyester thread came onto the scene and people were amazed at its strength and flexibility. A synthetic alternative to cotton, polyester is bright, smooth, and strong. It is also resistant to shrinkage and fading and leaves virtually no lint in your sewing machine. This type of thread is best for projects that need more strength and stretch.

## COTTON

Before the arrival of synthetic threads, cotton was king. The Mercerization process soon made cotton thread even more durable and colorfast. Cotton is still the top choice of many quilters and remains overwhelmingly popular. Quality cotton thread should be smooth to the touch and resist raveling. A good way to check the quality of cotton thread is to look at it closely to see if there are any bumps or flyaways. Soft and strong, cotton has a matte finish and wears well.

## THREAD WEIGHT

An easy rule of thumb with thread weight is the larger the number, the finer the thread. The most commonly used thread weight is 40. It's very versatile and can be used for just about anything. For piecing we like to use 50 weight thread. Fifty weight thread is great for bobbins and applique as well. If you'd like to put more emphasis on your applique, then go for a heavier 40 or 30 weight. Thicker thread is essential when hand quilting, so we recommend using 30 weight to avoid breakages. Finally, bright, strong polyester thread in 40 or 50 weight is perfect for machine embroidery and it has a nice sheen.

## MISSOURI STAR QUILT CO. THREAD

If you haven't tried MSQC thread yet, what are you waiting for? Choose from cotton or polyester in over 70 rich colors to coordinate with any project. This excellent thread can be used to quilt and sew a variety of fabrics, it runs smoothly through your sewing machine with a minimal amount of lint, and it can withstand the rigors of washing. Let your projects shine in the sunlight without fear, it has excellent sunlight resistance as well. Your memories are precious, so trust them to high quality thread at a great price and keep on stitching.

## JENNY DOAN'S HERITAGE COLLECTION BY AURIFIL

This collection came from a very special place, my childhood. I grew up in a Swedish home and I've always found inspiration in the beauty of my family's culture. Dala horses are a traditional symbol in Sweden, and for me they are a wonderful way to celebrate and remember my heritage. The colors of the Dala horse always remind me of happy times at home with my family. I'm thrilled to share these traditional colors with you.

## Quilt Tales
### - a quilt along story -

*Have you ever wondered what stories a quilt might tell? Do you find yourself daydreaming, longing for a little adventure? Let yourself be transported to a place outside of time and reality, and get lost in a magical world we've created just for you. Our favorite fairy tales have inspired us to create a unique quilting experience called "Quilt Tales." Each issue of BLOCK Magazine this year will contain a new chapter in a story to complement a quilt pattern. Stitch along with us and let your imagination run free!*

## The Forest Bride
### By Nichole Spravzoff

**BLOCK THREE**
SKOGSMARK

Early the next morning, Ingrid led Otto over to Marta's and then set out on her journey. From her small village it would take almost two days to travel by coach to Skogsmark, the ancient capitol of her homeland. It was a windy day with bursts of sunshine in between rain showers. Watching the tall pines swaying as the road jostled her made Ingrid feel hesitant to leave, but she gathered her thick woolen cloak around her shoulders and settled in despite her uncertainty, watching the road grow longer.

As the coach traveled along the forested road, Ingrid picked at a sewing project, putting in a few stitches here and there. The small squares made of blue and white cloth slowly came together to form an eight-pointed star, the shape of the Selburose, a traditional knitting design. It reminded her of a sweater her father had always worn.

After two days' journey, Ingrid finally neared her destination. Skogsmark was surrounded by a dense forest and the city spread out before her on the shore of a deeply flowing river. As the trees thinned, Ingrid could see plumes of smoke rising from chimneys atop stately brick buildings with oxidized, copper roofs. Seeing the city bathed in morning light was positively breathtaking, a striking contrast to the simple whitewashed cottages with thatched roofs in her village. It had been too long since she'd made an expedition to the city for the fabrics and notions needed for her craft and she had been making do with scant supplies.

Going to market alone made Ingrid feel like a child again. She recalled how her mother had deftly appraised fabrics, selecting only the finest, and negotiating a fair bargain with the merchants. It had seemed so easy to Ingrid as she tagged alongside her all those years. Now it felt as arduous as climbing a tall peak.

Within the hour, Ingrid arrived near the sprawling perimeter of the bazaar where she sprung down from the carriage without the aid of a gentleman and shouldered her satchel with ease. The driver shook his head as he watched her leave without a curtsy. Then he whistled, clicked his tongue at his horses, and cantered on, deeper into the center of the city.

When she passed a bakery, the scent of freshly baked cinnamon buns reached Ingrid's nose and she couldn't resist. Purchasing a roll with the change that clinked in her pocket, she sat on a bridge and paused for a moment to eat before entering the market. The blue-green water had swelled with the spring rainfall and the docks were lined with boats full of cargo. One boat in particular looked familiar. Ingrid looked closer and read the name on the prow, "Hansson." She swallowed uncomfortably. Could it be possible she had come to the city on the same day Karl and Gustav were delivering a timber shipment?

Before she could finish the last bite of cinnamon bun, she was interrupted by the noise coming from two men arguing beside the boat. As she edged closer, she realized she was staring right at Karl and an angry-looking merchant. Her suspicions were confirmed and she frowned, letting out an exasperated sigh. It seemed impossible to avoid her fate.

Desperately hoping she hadn't been seen, Ingrid dropped down beside the stone ledge until only her eyes peeked out over the top. In between horses clopping past, she caught snatches of their loud, unpleasant conversation.

Karl sounded outraged and desperate, "But you promised that you'd … "

The merchant's voice echoed over the water, " … shipment is far too small to repay your debts … can't overlook it this time …"

"You have no right! … soon I'll have my father's … " Karl snapped back.

Ingrid crept even closer, trying to decipher what was taking place. Looking back on Karl's confident demeanor at her cabin and seeing him today suddenly painted him as a completely different person. She had felt threatened by him then, but now she saw that he was in trouble and was begging for help. Pity washed over her, but as she continued to listen, her sympathy faded. Piecing together the conversation, she came to realize that Karl had been gambling away his earnings even more quickly than he made them.

Working for his father wasn't enough to cover his debts. He was determined to take control of the family business and have all the profits for himself, but Sven Hansson had made it clear that his sons would only inherit it if they were married. Karl didn't seem at all serious with anyone in the village and so Ingrid assumed that he was content to bide his time. Perhaps he would try to work out some other arrangement. Considering his predicament, he'd better figure out something fast. She cautiously waited for the exchange to end and then slipped away into the marketplace.

Ingrid strolled briskly past stalls filled with bushels of fruits and vegetables, sacks of grain, and fresh fish packed in ice, then imported spices in neat piles, dried herbs, household goods, and plush furs. When she finally reached the fabric merchants and caught her breath, she felt a wave of excitement wash over her. She was in her element.

Bright swaths of cloth hung overhead and bolts of fabric were stacked up like sheaves of wheat. Ingrid stood still for a moment, in awe of it all, unsure where to begin. She lightly fingered the selvage of a pretty calico. A thin-lipped woman in a starched white apron asked if she needed help and Ingrid shook her head, feeling suddenly overwhelmed. Then she gathered up her courage again and motioned the woman back over to ask for a few yards of the calicoes in various hues. They would make lovely summer dresses. Feeling more courageous, Ingrid ducked inside a large tent and called out to the shopkeeper. A man with a neatly trimmed white beard came out and greeted her warmly, "Good morning to you, dear girl. It's been some time."

Recognizing him from previous years, she smiled. "Hello, Peter. Yes, it has."

"Tell me, where is your mother today?" He grinned and looked about as if she might enter at any minute.

"My mother took ill some years ago." Ingrid looked down. "She's gone now."

"I had no idea. I'm so sorry. Agnes was a remarkable woman." He looked genuinely sad, even though he had not seen her for six years. Unsure of what to say next, he straightened a stack of fabric and then asked, "How can I help you today? I've just gotten in a shipment of linen from the Islands. Are you interested?" He chattered on to fill the silence.

Ingrid declined politely and handed him a carefully written list detailing the fabrics she needed.

Peter put on his spectacles and examined the request. "Shouldn't be a problem. I'll have your order ready for you shortly. Will you be taking it all along with you? There's quite a lot."

Ingrid thought for a moment and said, "I'll carry the smaller things. The rest of the supplies can be sent along on the next boat." They easily negotiated the price and she handed Peter a pouch of money.

He counted it without a second glance. "I hope it won't be too long before your next visit," he said.

Ingrid assured him that she would return soon and left the tent feeling lighter than air. It was so comforting to see a friendly face in a big city.

Winding her way through the stalls, Ingrid bought a variety of notions: sharp steel needles and pins, spools of cotton and silk thread, shell buttons, horn toggles, and even a few pieces of oiled leather. It was all piling up and her pack was becoming unwieldy. Even though she didn't have much money left, Ingrid stopped on a whim to admire some handsome, red leather clogs. They had a thick wooden sole and a heel to keep her feet out of the mud. They were absolutely perfect, but when she inquired about the price, her face fell and she carefully placed them back on the shelf. Thanking the shoemaker, she hastily turned to leave and ran face-first into the chest of a large, swaggering sailor. Apologizing profusely, Ingrid attempted to sidestep the oblivious man, who'd had a few too many pints of ale, and her heavy bag slipped off of her shoulder. It fell open, spilling its contents, and buttons went bouncing across the cobblestones.

In the bustling marketplace Ingrid's struggle seemed insignificant. She cried out and bent down to scoop up the precious buttons. But in her scramble to pick up her belongings before they were lost, she neglected to see a second pair of hands reach down and begin gathering up buttons alongside her. She started counting to see if she'd lost any and shook her head. Less than half were left. Then she heard someone say in a low voice, "Here are the rest." The voice sounded unfamiliar in the din of the crowd, but when she looked up to see who it was, she was astonished to see Gustav crouching next to her with a mound of buttons in his outstretched hand.

**to be continued...**

# variable star block

**BLOCK SIZE** 16" finished

**SUPPLY LIST**

(2) 10" dark blue #1 squares

(2) 10" dark blue #2 squares

(1) 10" medium blue square

(1) 10" medium dark blue square

(10) 10" white squares

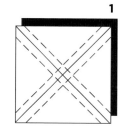

**1**

**3**

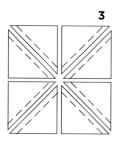

**5**

## 1 cut

From each of 4 white squares, cut: (4) 4½" squares for a **total of 16.**

## 2 draw, layer and sew

Draw a line from corner to corner twice on the diagonal on the reverse side of 6 white squares. Place a white square atop a blue square with right sides facing. Sew ¼" on either side of each of the drawn lines.

## 3 cut

Cut the sewn squares in half vertically and horizontally. Then cut on the drawn lines. Each set of sewn squares will yield 8 half-square triangles. A **total of 16** dark blue #1/white, **16** dark blue #2/white, **8** medium blue/white, and **8** medium dark blue/white are needed.

## 4 press and trim

Open each section to reveal a half-square triangle. Trim units to 4½".

## 5 block construction

Follow the diagram and sew the squares and half-square triangles together into 4 rows. Sew the rows together. **Make 4 blocks**, 2 will use the dark blue 1#/white half-square triangles on the outer edges and 2 will use the dark blue #2/white half-square triangles.

# all my xs

**QUILT SIZE**
69" X 78"

**BLOCK SIZE**
9" finished

**QUILT TOP**
1 package 10" print squares **or**
   4 matching packages of 5" print
   squares
4 yards background fabric – includes
   inner border

**OUTER BORDER**
1¼ yards

**BINDING**
¾ yard

**BACKING**
4¾ yards - vertical seam(s)

**SAMPLE QUILT**
**In the Limelight** by Wilmington
Batiks

**QUILTING PATTERN**
Flutterby

**ONLINE TUTORIALS**
msqc.co/blocksummer17

# cascade

**QUILT SIZE**
76½" X 89"

**BLOCK SIZE**
13½" x 4" finished

**QUILT TOP**
1 roll of 2½" print strips
1 roll of 2½" background strips
  **or** 3 yards background fabric
  cut into (40) 2½" x width of
  fabric strips

**BORDER**
1¼ yards

**BINDING**
¾ yard

**BACKING**
2½ yards 108" wide

**OTHER SUPPLIES**
The Binding Tool by TQM Products

**SAMPLE QUILT**
**Faded Memories** by Geri Robins for
Penny Rose Fabrics

**QUILTING PATTERN**
Simply Roses

**ONLINE TUTORIALS**
msqc.co/blocksummer17

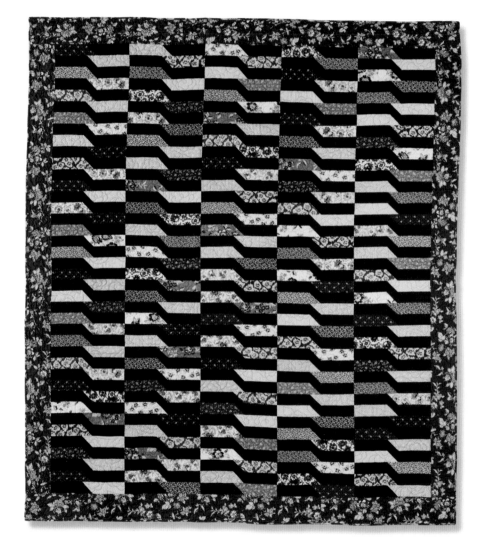

# dizzy daisy

**QUILT SIZE**
79" X 90"

**BLOCK SIZE**
9" finished

**QUILT TOP**
1 package 10" print squares **or**
  4 matching packages of 5" print
  squares
4¼ yards background fabric –
  includes inner border

**OUTER BORDER**
1¾ yards - includes cornerstones

**BINDING**
¾ yard

**BACKING**
7½ yards - vertical seam(s)

**SAMPLE QUILT**
**Early Bird** by Kate Spain for Moda
Fabrics

**QUILTING PATTERN**
Flutterby

**ONLINE TUTORIALS**
msqc.co/blocksummer17

# emerald isle

**QUILT SIZE**
79" X 95"

**BLOCK SIZE**
4" x 8" finished

**QUILT TOP**
1 package 10" print squares
1 package 10" background squares

**INNER BORDER**
¾ yard

**OUTER BORDER**
1¾ yards

**BINDING**
¾ yard

**BACKING**
3 yards - 90" wide

**SAMPLE QUILT**
**Bon Voyage** by My KT for Windham
Fabrics

**QUILTING PATTERN**
Meander

**ONLINE TUTORIALS**
msqc.co/blocksummer17

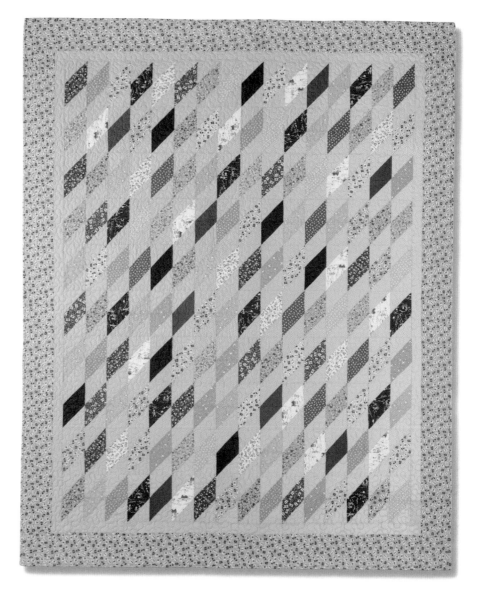

# kindred pinwheel

**QUILT SIZE**
91" x 104"

**BLOCK SIZE**
11" finished

**QUILT TOP**
1 package 10" print squares
3¾ yards background fabric
2½ yards dark solid – sashing
½ yard medium solid – cornerstones

**BORDER**
1¾ yards

**BINDING**
1 yard

**BACKING**
8½ yards - horizonal seam(s)

**OTHER SUPPLIES**
Bloc_Loc Ruler

**SAMPLE QUILT**
**Sand In My Shoes** by McKenna Ryan
for Robert Kaufman

**QUILTING PATTERN**
Flutterby

**ONLINE TUTORIALS**
msqc.co/blocksummer17

# ribbon dance

**QUILT SIZE**
78" X 86"

**BLOCK SIZE**
8" x 12" finished

**QUILT TOP**
1 package 10" print squares
1 package 10" background squares

**INNER BORDER**
¾ yard

**OUTER BORDER**
1½ yards

**BINDING**
¾ yard

**BACKING**
7¼ yards - horizontal seam(s)

**SAMPLE QUILT**
**Linen and Lawn** by Sue Daley for
Riley Blake Designs

**QUILTING PATTERN**
Champagne Bubbles

**ONLINE TUTORIALS**
msqc.co/blocksummer17

# small dashing stars

**QUILT SIZE**
56½" X 56½"

**BLOCK SIZE**
10½" finished

**QUILT TOP**
2 matching packages 5" print squares
2 yards background fabric

**BORDER**
1¼ yard – includes squares used in blocks and cornerstones

**BINDING**
¾ yard

**BACKING**
3¾ yards - vertical seam(s)

**SAMPLE QUILT**
**Sunday Supper** by Sweetwater for Moda Fabrics

**QUILTING PATTERN**
Loops & Swirls

**ONLINE TUTORIALS**
msqc.co/blocksummer17

# summer notes

**QUILT SIZE**
78″ X 86″

**BLOCK SIZE**
8″ x 12″ finished

**QUILT TOP**
1 package 10″ print squares
1 package 10″ background
   squares

**INNER BORDER**
¾ yard

**OUTER BORDER**
1½ yards

**BINDING**
¾ yard

**BACKING**
7¼ yards - horizontal seam(s)

**SAMPLE QUILT**
**Linen and Lawn** by Sue Daley for
Riley Blake Designs

**QUILTING PATTERN**
Arc Doodle

**ONLINE TUTORIALS**
msqc.co/blocksummer17

# tender hearts

**QUILT SIZE**
72" X 77"

**BLOCK SIZE**
9" x 8" finished

**QUILT TOP**
1 roll of 2½" strips
2½ yards background fabric –
    includes inner border and
    cornerstones
1½ yards contrasting solid -
    sashing rectangles

**OUTER BORDER**
1½ yards

**BINDING**
¾ yard

**BACKING**
4¾ yards - vertical seam(s)

**SAMPLE QUILT**
**Kona Cotton Solids Blushing
Bouquet Palette** by RK Studios for
Robert Kaufman

**QUILTING PATTERN**
Large Hearts

**ONLINE TUTORIALS**
msqc.co/blocksummer17

# under construction

**QUILT SIZE**
69" X 91"

**BLOCK SIZE**
4½" x 9½" finished

**QUILT TOP**
1 package 10" print squares
3 yards background fabric

**INNER BORDER**
¾ yard

**OUTER BORDER**
1½ yards

**BINDING**
¾ yard

**BACKING**
5½ yards - vertical seam(s)

**SAMPLE QUILT**
**Big Dig** by Whistler Studios for
Windham Fabrics

**QUILTING PATTERN**
Meander

**ONLINE TUTORIALS**
msqc.co/blocksummer17

# construction basics

## general quilting

- All seams are ¼" inch unless directions specify differently.
- Cutting instructions are given at the point when cutting is required.
- Precuts are not prewashed; therefore do not prewash other fabrics in the project.
- All strips are cut width of fabric.
- Remove all selvages.

## press seams

- Use a steam iron on the cotton setting.
- Press the seam just as it was sewn right sides together. This "sets" the seam.
- With dark fabric on top, lift the dark fabric and press back.
- The seam allowance is pressed toward the dark side. Some patterns may direct otherwise for certain situations.
- Follow pressing arrows in the diagrams when indicated.
- Press toward borders. Pieced borders may demand otherwise.
- Press diagonal seams open on binding to reduce bulk.

## borders

- Always measure the quilt top 3 times before cutting borders.
- Start measuring about 4" in from each side and through the center vertically.
- Take the average of those 3 measurements.
- Cut 2 border strips to that size. Piece strips together if needed.
- Attach one to either side of the quilt.

- Position the border fabric on top as you sew. The feed dogs can act like rufflers. Having the border on top will prevent waviness and keep the quilt straight.
- Repeat this process for the top and bottom borders, measuring the width 3 times.
- Include the newly attached side borders in your measurements.
- Press toward the borders.

## binding

*find a video tutorial at: www.msqc.co/006*

- Use 2½" strips for binding.
- Sew strips end-to-end into one long strip with diagonal seams, aka the plus sign method (next). Press seams open.
- Fold in half lengthwise wrong sides together and press.
- The entire length should equal the outside dimension of the quilt plus 15" - 20."

## plus sign method

- Lay one strip across the other as if to make a plus sign right sides together.
- Sew from top inside to bottom outside corners crossing the intersections of fabric as you sew. Trim excess to ¼" seam allowance.
- Press seam open.

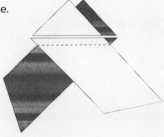

*find a video tutorial at: www.msqc.co/001*

# attach binding

- Match raw edges of folded binding to the quilt top edge.
- Leave a 10" tail at the beginning.
- Use a ¼" seam allowance.
- Start in the middle of a long straight side.

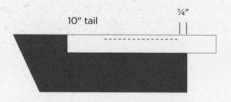

10" tail      ¼"

# miter corners

- Stop sewing ¼" before the corner.
- Move the quilt out from under the presser foot.
- Clip the threads.
- Flip the binding up at a 90° angle to the edge just sewn.
- Fold the binding down along the next side to be sewn, aligning raw edges.
- The fold will lie along the edge just completed.
- Begin sewing on the fold.

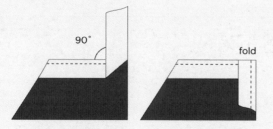

90°      fold

# close binding

*MSQC recommends* The Binding Tool from TQM Products to finish binding perfectly every time.

- Stop sewing when you have 12" left to reach the start.
- Where the binding tails come together, trim excess leaving only 2½" of overlap.
- It helps to pin or clip the quilt together at the two points where the binding starts and stops. This takes the pressure off of the binding tails while you work.
- Use the plus sign method to sew the two binding ends together, except this time when making the plus sign, match the edges. Using a pencil, mark your sewing line because you won't be able to see where the corners intersect. Sew across.

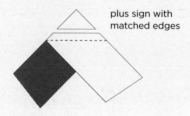

plus sign with matched edges

- Trim off excess; press seam open.
- Fold in half wrong sides together, and align all raw edges to the quilt top.
- Sew this last binding section to the quilt. Press.
- Turn the folded edge of the binding around to the back of the quilt and tack into place with an invisible stitch or machine stitch if you wish.